Not Another
Cookbook

Susan Schurr

with Betsy Rush, R.D.

DEDICATION

To Nana

You feed my soul with wisdom, guidance, inspiration and endless love.
I will never grow hungry, for you are the nourishment of my being.

Cover, design and illustrations by Laurie Burton.

Printed by Leopold Graphics.

ISBN: 0-9747050-0-4

To order additional copies of this book, please contact Susan Schurr at:

SUSAN.SCHURR@GMAIL.COM

GRATITUDE

As other authors have said, a book is a collaborative effort by many people giving their time, enthusiasm and special talents. I would like to thank all of those people in my life who have been instrumental in helping to make this project a reality. Your advice, input and sharing of recipes have been invaluable.

To my great friend, Jane Goldstein, I want to thank you for all of the work that you did to create *Not Another Cookbook*. Your meal suggestions, recipes and tips were so helpful. I enjoyed every minute that we spent together on this project.

To Laurie Burton, thank you, thank you, and thank you again. Your gift for graphic design is amazing. I love your creativity, energy and flexibility. You have talent and wisdom beyond your years.

To Betsy Rush, thank you for your nutritional expertise. I loved reviewing the menu plans with you. Your attitude of "everything in moderation" appeals to so many people. You have been such an asset to this book.

To Larry Altman, thank you for your list of clever book titles, marketing ideas, and introducing me to Laurie. Your knowledge of promotion, along with your sense of humor, makes working with you so much fun.

To Glenda Daulerio, thank you for being my editor. Your words of wisdom have not only influenced this book, but my life as well. I thank you.

To my parents and in-laws, thank you for providing me with memories of many meals filled with laughter and smiles. You have taught me not only the importance of supplying good food to my family, but also sitting down with them to enjoy it.

To my sons, thank you for your patience. You were wonderful taste testers and food critics, and I promise you now that the book is finished we can have fast food - *on occasion*.

To my loving husband, thank you for your guidance and support of every project I undertake. You are my true inspiration in life.

Tired of Take Out

Face it, we're busier than ever. With the increase in two working-parent families and single-parent families, as well as the availability of more after-school activities, many of us find it difficult to get a healthy meal on the table, let alone have the time to sit down and enjoy it together. For some of us, our afternoons are consumed with shuttling kids from school to soccer practice, from swim meets to religious school, and from music lessons to the orthodontist. As we all know walking in the door with starving, tired kids is not the time to begin thinking about what to have for dinner.

Because of my frustration - and guilt - over too many dinners of cold cereal and fast food drive-thru, I had to find a better way. I have devised this meal planning *system* which allows me to provide healthier meals for my family. I am not a gourmet cook or a professional chef; I am a typical mom who was tired of take out. I have created this simple meal planner with the help of registered dietitian Betsy Rush and have been successfully using it for almost two years. I know my family is now eating healthier, balanced meals, and I am less stressed at dinner time.

Think Outside the Box

If you're like me, you tend to make the same meals for your family week after week. If it's Thursday, it must be spaghetti for dinner. To help make your life easier and give your family a little variety, this book supplies you with ideas for 52 weeks of breakfasts, lunches, snacks, and choices for either leisurely dinners or quick dinners. The meal ideas are merely suggestions. Feel free to mix and match entreés with side dishes, substituting your favorite vegetable and creating your own meals. Many kids seem to enjoy having breakfast for dinner. Just as there's nothing wrong with having scrambled eggs as your evening meal, having a turkey sandwich in the morning before work or school makes a very nutritious breakfast. Have fun with this meal planner. You may even want to have your kids help plan the meals.

Our recommendation, however, is that you try as much as possible to:

1) Include whole grains and whole grain breads in your meals.
2) Choose skim or 1% milk, part-skim cheeses as well as other reduced-fat dairy items.
3) Use fresh or frozen fruits and vegetables rather than canned.
4) Plan to include fish at least once or twice a week.
5) Occasionally substitute soy-based cheeses and meats as an alternative to dairy and animal products.
6) Each week buy and serve a fruit, vegetable or grain that your family may have never tried.
7) Offer a fruit and/or vegetable at each meal and snack to help achieve the recommended five a day.

NOTE: This book is not intended to provide medical advice or be a substitute for the advice from your personal physician. Readers are advised to consult their own doctors or other qualified health professionals regarding their own dietary needs.

This is *Not Another Cookbook*, but...

...there are some recipes for you to try. Some of the more unique menu items can be found in the "Recipes" section. These items are marked on your weekly meal planner with the page number on which the recipe can be found. The other menu items are more common and can be found in many basic cookbooks or on the internet.

Let's Begin

Step One

Briefly skim through the planner to familiarize yourself with its contents. You will see that it has been divided into 52 weeks of meal plans by seasons. In each season there are three months or thirteen weeks. Autumn includes the months September, October and November. Winter consists of December, January and February. The spring season is March, April and May and summer is the months June, July and August.

The intention is to allow you to begin the planner any time of the year you choose. Just flip to the appropriate season and begin. The sample meal plans contain menu ideas using the freshest fruits and vegetables for each season.

Step Two

Find the section entitled "Favorites" and list some of the foods that you and your family particularly like. This list will help when you are planning your weekly meals. Continue to add items to this section throughout the year as you create new meals that your family enjoys.

Step Three

After looking at your weekly activities, decide which evenings you can have a leisurely dinner and which evenings you will need to make something quick.

Step Four

Read the weekly menu suggestions. If any of the breakfast, lunch, snack or dinner ideas appeal to you, transpose them onto your personalized weekly meal plan on the following page. Do this for every day of that week. For those suggested meals that you do not care for, substitute a meal that you and your family would prefer. You can flip back to the "Favorites" section to remind you of meals your family enjoyed.

Step Five

Locate the "Market" section. Create a list of groceries that you are going to need for the coming week. When you are ready to go to the market, just tear off your personal shopping list and away you go. Food shopping can be a bit of a chore for some, so don't forget to read the inspirational messages and tips on the back of the shopping lists.

Step Six

All right, now you're back from the market. After you unpack your groceries, cut up some fruits and vegetables and place them in storage containers or plastic bags if you have time. Once refrigerated, these fruits and vegetables are ready for your kid's afternoon snack or as the part of a quick salad to have with dinner.

Give it a try...

I hope this meal planning *system* will be helpful to you. Give it a try. It's simple.

In good health,

SS

FAVORITES

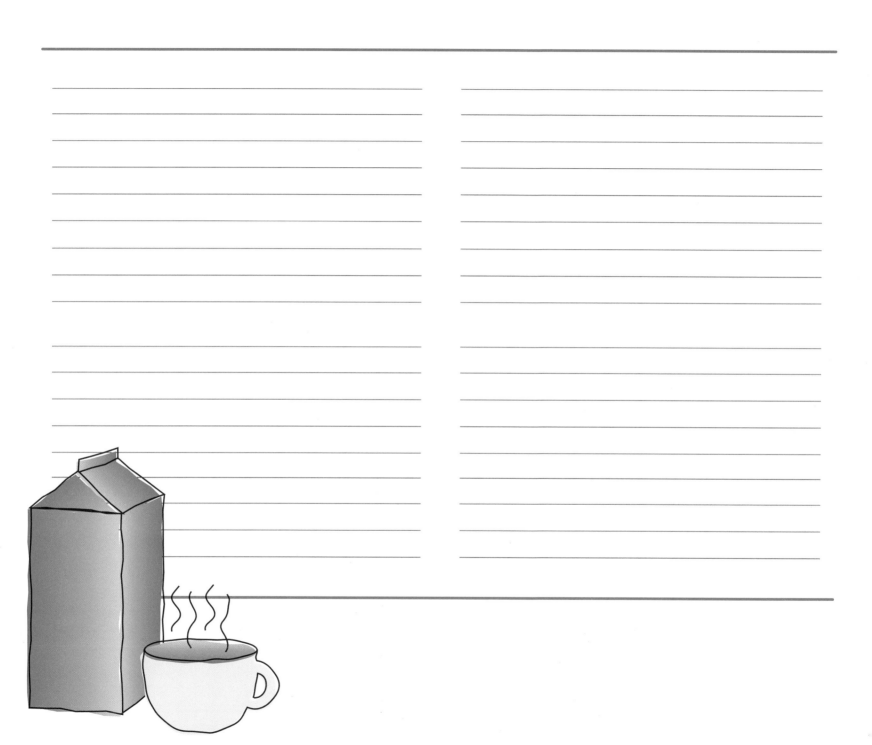

_____

_____   _____
_____   _____
_____   _____
_____   _____
_____   _____
_____   _____
_____   _____
_____   _____
_____   _____
_____   _____
_____   _____
_____   _____
_____   _____
_____   _____

FAVORITES

Quick Dinner

	MONDAY	TUESDAY	WEDNESDAY	THURSDAY	FRIDAY	SATURDAY	SUNDAY
BREAKFAST	Pumpkin muffins [10] spread with peanut butter orange wedges	scrambled eggs on toasted English muffin with cheese grapes	warm cream of wheat with sliced bananas sprinkled with cinnamon sugar	grilled cheese with ham and tomato	whole-grain cold cereal with soy milk half grapefruit	cubed turkey and cheese kabob strawberries	smoked salmon and cream cheese omelette toasted bagel cantaloupe wedge
LUNCH	turkey breast on a bagel with thousand island dressing carrots and celery sticks	tuna salad on whole-grain bread with shredded carrots	clam chowder whole-grain crackers apple	deviled eggs onion roll clementine	beef salami and Havarti cheese slices champagne mustard sesame crackers carrot sticks	veggie burger on a whole-grain bun with lettuce and tomato	almond butter and fruit jam on whole-grain bread
SNACK	apple wedges dipped in honey	hot chocolate graham crackers	pear slices dipped in yogurt	cold veggies with salsa	dried apricots and pineapple	cucumber spears and tortilla chips with veggie dip [2]	mango slices
DINNER	Crispy Dijon Chicken [17] orzo with diced red peppers salad	Tomato-Spinach Risotto [15] salad	beef and vegetable kabobs baked potatoes salad	Chicken Cutlets with Smoked Turkey and Fontina [16] apple-cranberry stuffing, broccoli	Salmon with Red Onions [26] wild rice with mushrooms steamed green beans	vegetable Lasagna [15] salad garlic bread	Pork tenderloin roast, peas Sweet Potato and Apple Casserole [31] pears
QUICK DINNER	Capered Chicken Cutlets [16] salad	Baked Burritos [12] avocado and tomato salad	sloppy joe on a sesame seed bun sauteed spinach	sliced smoked turkey wrap with arugula and cranberry relish	Oven-Baked Fried Fish [25] potato puffs red pepper slices	angel hair pasta with diced tomatoes salad topped with goat cheese and pecans, garlic bread	Puffed Pancake [10] with sauteed bananas

	MONDAY	TUESDAY	WEDNESDAY	THURSDAY	FRIDAY	SATURDAY	SUNDAY
BREAKFAST							
LUNCH							
SNACK							
DINNER							
QUICK DINNER							

	MONDAY	TUESDAY	WEDNESDAY	THURSDAY	FRIDAY	SATURDAY	SUNDAY
BREAKFAST	warm oatmeal sprinkled with raisins and nutmeg kiwi slices	Energy Muffin 8 orange wedges	egg white omelette with soy cheese grapes	Baked Apples 5 topped with pecans and drizzled with honey	low-fat goat cheese spread on rice cakes pear slices	toasted pumpernickel bagel spread with pumpkin butter clementine	Pancakes with maple syrup orange juice
LUNCH	Cream Cheese and Salsa Wrap 8	roast beef on rye with coleslaw	Peanut butter and fruit jam tea sandwiches vegetable soup	lean ham roll-ups dipped in yellow mustard granola bar	chicken noodle soup Carrot Muffin 6	turkey and Provolone hoagie with sweet peppers	mixed greens with crumbled feta cheese and Kalamata olives
SNACK	warm apple cider popcorn	cold veggies with low-fat sour cream onion dip	tomato juice whole edamame (frozen soybeans)	half grapefruit whole-grain crackers	grapes	banana slices topped with cashew butter	sushi salad with ginger dressing
DINNER	cornish game hen wild rice Honey-Ginger Carrots 29	Light Crab Cakes 24 on toast with yellow pepper rings sauteed spinach with garlic	stuffed shells with tomato sauce Caesar salad Italian bread	Lemon Chicken 17 mashed sweet potatoes snow pea pods	Osso Buco 21 (veal shanks) egg noodles salad	broiled mahi-mahi acorn squash steamed broccoli	vegetarian chili warm cornbread muffins half grapefruit
QUICK DINNER	deli turkey and cranberry sauce wrap	Fresh Tuna Burgers 24 raw baby carrots	Penne with mushroom marinara sauce Italian bread salad	chicken and veggie stir-fry Jasmine rice	tofu chili dog apple sauce	sauteed veal patties served in a pita with lettuce and tomato, drizzled with cucumber yogurt sauce	Couscous Salad with Beans and Greens 12

	MONDAY	TUESDAY	WEDNESDAY	THURSDAY	FRIDAY	SATURDAY	SUNDAY
BREAKFAST							
LUNCH							
SNACK							
DINNER							
QUICK DINNER							

	MONDAY	TUESDAY	WEDNESDAY	THURSDAY	FRIDAY	SATURDAY	SUNDAY
BREAKFAST	challah French toast with powdered sugar sliced apple	Peanut butter and crunchy granola on whole-grain bread melon wedge	buckwheat hot cereal sprinkled with raisins and cinnamon sugar	yogurt with orange sections toasted English muffin with fruit preserves	whole-grain cold cereal with sliced bananas and soy milk	Cheddar Cornmeal Waffle with Salsa 6 Pear	Hole in One Eggs 8 veggie bacon pineapple chunks
LUNCH	turkey bologna on whole-grain bread with lettuce, tomato and mustard	hummus in a whole wheat pita with cucumber and tomato slices	egg salad on a croissant with lettuce	turkey breast slices wrapped around carrot sticks dipped in honey mustard	tuna salad with diced apples on raisin bread	hot dogs crescent rolls clementine	minestrone soup crusty roll
SNACK	carrot sticks tortilla chips with guacamole	cold veggies with ranch dressing	banana bread glass of milk	a handful of mixed nuts veggie juice	graham crackers with fruit jam	celery stuffed with cream cheese topped with almonds	apple sauce sprinkled with cinnamon
DINNER	Scallops with Almonds 26 brown rice steamed green beans	Sweet and Sour Meatballs 22 egg noodles salad	veal piccata couscous broiled tomatoes	Poached salmon mashed potatoes broccoli with black olives	vegetable stew	chicken cacciatore fusilli pasta Italian bread	Homemade Fried Rice 13 salad with ginger dressing
QUICK DINNER	Make Your Own Pizza: sauteed bay scallops and veggies	tacos shredded cheese, shredded lettuce and sour cream	chicken and cheese quesadilla	tomato soup shrimp cocktail crusty bread	veggie stir-fry with cashews	hot turkey sandwich with gravy raw baby carrots	Pierogies Pesto 14 salad

	BREAKFAST	LUNCH	SNACK	DINNER	QUICK DINNER
MONDAY					
TUESDAY					
WEDNESDAY					
THURSDAY					
FRIDAY					
SATURDAY					
SUNDAY					

	MONDAY	TUESDAY	WEDNESDAY	THURSDAY	FRIDAY	SATURDAY	SUNDAY
BREAKFAST	cinnamon raisin bagel spread with soy cream cheese and blueberry jam	warm oatmeal with a pat of butter sliced strawberries	whole-grain crackers topped with cashew butter half grapefruit	Poached egg on an English muffin clementine	whole-grain cold cereal with sliced bananas	orange and grapefruit sections topped with yogurt and walnuts	Cottage Cheese Pancakes [7] topped with sauteed apples
LUNCH	chicken vegetable soup apple and cheddar cheese wedges	cubed lean ham and fruit kabob country biscuit	mixed greens topped with tuna salad	vanilla yogurt sprinkled with Homemade Trail Mix [8] pear	cottage cheese and sliced strawberries	shrimp salad on an onion roll tangelo	egg salad and cucumber slices on a bagel
SNACK	hard-boiled egg whole-grain crackers red pepper slices	popcorn drizzled with olive oil and garlic powder apple cider	oatbran muffin veggie juice	cold veggies with Cucumber Dip [1]	Peanut butter and jam on whole-grain crackers	bagel chips with herbed cream cheese spread carrot and celery sticks	banana slices dipped in melted chocolate
DINNER	swordfish with diced tomatoes and capers orzo pasta	Teriyaki London Broil [23] scalloped potatoes sugar snap peas	Butternut Squash Soup [3] Italian bread salad Baked Apples [5]	sauteed turkey cutlets barley creamed spinach	Roasted Potatoes Topped with Sun-Dried Tomato Pesto [30] salad	chicken curry rice salad	apricot glazed baked ham candied sweet potatoes steamed green beans
QUICK DINNER	Linguini with Shrimp Scampi [25] salad	Zesty Barbecue Pitas [23] raw cauliflower florets	gnocchi with roasted peppers and garlic salad	turkey bacon, lettuce and tomato on French bread	tofu stir-fry	chicken steak on a long roll with tomato sauce and fried onions	turkey hot dogs baked beans coleslaw

	QUICK DINNER	DINNER	SNACK	LUNCH	BREAKFAST
MONDAY					
TUESDAY					
WEDNESDAY					
THURSDAY					
FRIDAY					
SATURDAY					
SUNDAY					

	MONDAY	TUESDAY	WEDNESDAY	THURSDAY	FRIDAY	SATURDAY	SUNDAY
BREAKFAST	multi-grain hot cereal topped with raisins and nutmeg	cheese quesadilla orange wedges	whole-grain waffle with almond butter and sliced bananas	Cheese Blintzes [7] topped with powdered sugar mango slices	scrambled eggs pumpernickel toast pear	yogurt topped with fruit lemon scone	egg white omelette whole-grain toast half grapefruit
LUNCH	smoked turkey and muenster cheese cubes dipped in champagne mustard grapes	cold veggies dipped in hummus pita chips	tuna salad with shredded carrots on a French baguette	chicken salad hoagie baby carrots	cream cheese and jam tea sandwiches grapes	roast beef and Swiss cheese on rye bread with thousand island dressing mandarin oranges	onion soup with croutons apple
SNACK	graham crackers hot chocolate	Baked Apples [5] with cinnamon and pecans	Zucchini Bread [11] half grapefruit	warm apple cider a handful of mixed nuts	pineapple and kiwi slices	whole-grain bread sticks grapes	peanut butter stuffed celery rolled in raisins
DINNER	fettuccini with broccoli and shrimp	Squash and Chard Chili [22] salad	chicken Kiev bowtie pasta sauteed spinach	wild mushroom risotto salad clementine	steamed red snapper Corn Pudding [29] steamed green beans	roasted turkey breast stuffing peas cranberry sauce	spaghetti and Tiny Meatballs [23] salad garlic bread
QUICK DINNER	Shrimp Wrap with Corn Salsa [26]	hot deli roast beef sandwich with gravy instant mashed potatoes steamed carrots	chicken noodle soup crusty bread salad	bean and cheese enchiladas radishes	Grilled Fresh Tuna Salad [24]	deli turkey breast on a roll with cranberry sauce	Make Your Own Pizza: Mexican [13]

QUICK DINNER

DINNER

SNACK

LUNCH

BREAKFAST

MONDAY

TUESDAY

WEDNESDAY

THURSDAY

FRIDAY

SATURDAY

SUNDAY

	MONDAY	TUESDAY	WEDNESDAY	THURSDAY	FRIDAY	SATURDAY	SUNDAY
BREAKFAST	blueberry scones with jam	cinnamon raisin French toast with maple syrup tangelo	Baked Apples 5 sprinkled with granola	warm cream of wheat with a swirl of honey sliced strawberries	pineapple and strawberry yogurt smoothie blueberry muffin	whole-grain cold cereal with sliced bananas	buttermilk waffles Canadian bacon clementine
LUNCH	cottage cheese topped with diced pear and sprinkled with almonds whole-grain crackers	lean ham and cheese hoagie	roasted eggplant spread pita triangles	corned beef on rye with coleslaw and Russian dressing	Warm Carrot Soup 4 salad	veggie burger on a whole-grain bun with lettuce, tomato and a pickle	smoked salmon tea sandwiches with herbed cream cheese pineapple chunks
SNACK	cold veggies with White Bean Dip 2	banana slices dipped in yogurt	cheddar cheese wedge grapes	red pepper slices and cauliflower florets with ranch dressing	egg rolls	Cranberry Bread 7 spread with cream cheese granny smith apple	apple sauce with cinnamon
DINNER	broiled salmon buttered noodles salad	Oriental Chicken Kabobs 18 with rice cucumber salad	broiled lamb chops Roasted Root Vegetables 30 salad	four-cheese ravioli with garlic tomato sauce salad Italian bread	flounder and broccoli roll-ups basmati rice	baked chicken acorn squash with pecans and maple syrup steamed green beans	Standing Rib Roast 22 mashed potatoes with gravy peas glazed carrots
QUICK DINNER	shrimp chowder salad	Pasta Chicken Caesar Salad 18	Turkey Meatball Sub 19 lettuce wedge	angel hair pasta with pesto sauce salad	crab quesadillas cantaloupe cubes	chef's salad	sloppy joe on a poppy seed bun raw baby carrots

	BREAKFAST	LUNCH	SNACK	DINNER	QUICK DINNER
MONDAY					
TUESDAY					
WEDNESDAY					
THURSDAY					
FRIDAY					
SATURDAY					
SUNDAY					

	MONDAY	TUESDAY	WEDNESDAY	THURSDAY	FRIDAY	SATURDAY	SUNDAY
BREAKFAST	warm oatmeal with chopped apples and dates	Pumpkin muffin 10 spread with almond butter orange wedges	fried eggs whole-grain toast with Peach butter watermelon chunks	fruit kabob a handful of mixed nuts	whole-grain cold cereal with sliced strawberries	raisin toast with sliced apple and melted soy cheese	Puffed Pancake 10 drizzled with maple syrup banana
LUNCH	beef salami cubes with grainy mustard celery sticks	turkey wrap with cucumber, red pepper rings and Dijon mustard	Tomato and Bean Soup 4 whole-grain bread	garden salad with flaked tuna beef vegetable soup	lean ham and cheddar cheese on a country biscuit carrot salad	sushi salad with ginger dressing	grilled cheese with fresh mozzarella, tomato and basil on sourdough bread pear
SNACK	Popcorn Balls 10	cold veggies and onion dip	warm apple cider graham crackers with jam	Cream Cheese and Salsa Wrap 8	banana slices dipped in yogurt and sprinkled with wheat germ	oatmeal cookie glass of milk	hot chocolate with marshmallows
DINNER	Pot roasted chicken with carrots and potatoes salad	Mac and Cheese 13 salad	meatloaf corn and peas salad	chicken stir-fry brown rice honeydew cubes	bouillabaisse roasted new potatoes and asparagus crusty bread	Tomato-Spinach Risotto 15 sauteed shrimp salad	veal stew barley peasant bread
QUICK DINNER	hot deli turkey sandwich with gravy steamed broccoli	elbow noodles with cottage cheese pear	tacos shredded cheese, shredded lettuce and sour cream	sauteed chicken cutlets topped with sun-dried tomatoes and provolone cheese on focaccia bread	seafood salad topped with mandarin oranges over lettuce	Pasta Frittata 9 apple sauce	white beans with olive oil salad orange and grapefruit sections

	QUICK DINNER
	DINNER
	SNACK
	LUNCH
	BREAKFAST

MONDAY

TUESDAY

WEDNESDAY

THURSDAY

FRIDAY

SATURDAY

SUNDAY

	MONDAY	TUESDAY	WEDNESDAY	THURSDAY	FRIDAY	SATURDAY	SUNDAY
BREAKFAST	Peanut butter, jam and granola wrap Pear	Hole in One Eggs 8 orange wedges	multi-grain hot cereal topped with sliced bananas and soy milk	whole-grain waffles spread with pumpkin butter grapefruit sections	challah French toast with powdered sugar and sauteed pears	cottage cheese topped with sliced strawberries	honeydew wedge topped with a dollop of vanilla yogurt and sprinkled with almonds
LUNCH	lentil soup whole wheat crackers grapes	roast beef on an onion roll with horseradish sauce celery sticks	smoked turkey and Havarti cheese on French bread with lettuce and grainy mustard cantaloupe wedge	muenster cheese on raisin bread with apple slices and lettuce	hummus wrap with lettuce, tomato and cucumbers	turkey bologna on rye toast with lettuce, tomato and mustard	mixed green salad with crumbled goat cheese and tomatoes
SNACK	apple wedge dipped in honey	Pita triangles with eggplant dip	cold veggies with thousand island dressing	veggie sticks veggie pepperoni wheat crackers	Carrot Muffin 6 sliced apple	pineapple chunks	Peanut butter cookie glass of milk
DINNER	broiled tilapia buttered new potatoes steamed green beans	Black Beans and Rice 12 avocado and tomato salad	spaghetti with tomato sauce salad Italian bread	barbecued chicken couscous creamed spinach	beef brisket noodle pudding Honey-Ginger Carrots 29	Salmon Baked in Foil 25 basmati rice sauteed shredded zucchini	southern fried chicken garlic mashed potatoes steamed broccoli buttermilk biscuits
QUICK DINNER	Oven-Baked Fried Fish 25 on a kaiser roll with tartar sauce steamed escarole	Baked Burritos 12 avocado and tomato salad	gnocchi with butter and sprinkled with Parmesan cheese and walnuts celery and carrot sticks	Chicken Fajitas 16 sour cream and salsa	Make Your Own Pizza: cheese burger pizza	canned salmon salad on whole-grain toast cucumber salad	Fast and Easy Chicken Chili 17 cornbread apple sauce

QUICK DINNER

DINNER

SNACK

LUNCH

BREAKFAST

MONDAY

TUESDAY

WEDNESDAY

THURSDAY

FRIDAY

SATURDAY

SUNDAY

	MONDAY	TUESDAY	WEDNESDAY	THURSDAY	FRIDAY	SATURDAY	SUNDAY
BREAKFAST	whole-grain cold cereal with chopped prunes	hard-boiled egg whole-grain bagel spread with pear butter	warm buckwheat cereal with milk apple sauce	peanut butter and banana sandwich on whole-grain bread	English muffin pizza	sliced pears with maple yogurt 9	fried eggs turkey sausage pumpernickel toast half grapefruit
LUNCH	shrimp salad on sourdough bread with lettuce apple	almond butter and strawberry preserves wrap	roast beef and provolone cheese hoagie honeydew cubes	tuna with diced apples on raisin bread	cubed turkey pineapple and grape kabob	veggie quesadilla mango slices	potato soup spinach salad crusty bread
SNACK	cantaloupe chunks topped with a scoop of cottage cheese	celery stuffed with cream cheese topped with raisins	fruit smoothie graham crackers	chocolate or vanilla soy pudding	fig bar glass of milk	a handful of mixed nuts veggie juice	whole-grain crackers topped with cream cheese and olive spread mandarin oranges
DINNER	broiled veal chops baked acorn squash lima beans	tuna noodle casserole salad	Lemon Chicken 17 wild rice broccoli with black olives	spaghetti with turkey meatballs crusty bread Baked Apples 5	monkfish with lemon butter roasted potatoes salad	leg of lamb brown rice steamed green beans	chicken pot pie sliced tomatoes and cucumbers
QUICK DINNER	veal patty on a sesame bun with cucumber, lettuce and tomato	Tuna Melt 27 lettuce wedge pickles olives	Turkey (or chicken) Enchilada 19 quick brown rice salad	angel hair pasta with diced tomatoes cucumber spears	tofu and mixed veggie stir-fry	sauteed minute steaks with melted provolone cheese on Italian bread salad	deli turkey breast on raisin toast with cranberry sauce

	QUICK DINNER	DINNER	SNACK	LUNCH	BREAKFAST
MONDAY					
TUESDAY					
WEDNESDAY					
THURSDAY					
FRIDAY					
SATURDAY					
SUNDAY					

	MONDAY	TUESDAY	WEDNESDAY	THURSDAY	FRIDAY	SATURDAY	SUNDAY
BREAKFAST	Cranberry Bread [7] spread with almond butter and topped with raisins	oatmeal with pecans and sliced bananas	orange and grapefruit sections topped with yogurt and walnuts	whole-grain waffles with maple syrup sliced pear	Plain yogurt topped with sliced strawberries, sprinkled with wheat germ	French toast with honey	smoked salmon and cream cheese on a bagel with sliced tomato kiwi slices
LUNCH	smoked turkey and dilled Havarti cheese roll-ups multi-grain crackers grapes	chicken noodle soup whole-grain crackers cantaloupe wedge	egg salad wrap with lettuce and tomato	fruit salad whole-grain crackers with peanut butter	chicken salad with grapes on pumpernickel bread	tortilla chips sprinkled with Monterey Jack cheese and beans, broiled or microwaved salsa	Pierogi Nicoise Salad [25]
SNACK	carrot sticks with Hot Bean Dip [1]	cottage cheese topped with crushed pineapple	veggie sticks and bagel chips with hummus	whole edamame (frozen soybeans) veggie juice	hot chocolate with whipped cream banana	dried apricots	cold veggies with ranch dressing
DINNER	cheese ravioli with marinara sauce salad Italian bread	salmon cakes Jasmine rice broiled tomato	roasted turkey breast mashed sweet potatoes steamed green beans	vegetable Lasagna [15] salad	seafood stew corn steamed broccoli	chicken cordon bleu couscous asparagus	Hearty Pasta Saute [21] pineapple cubes
QUICK DINNER	jelly crepes with powdered sugar clementine	grilled tuna kabobs with tomatoes, onions and potatoes	turkey hot dogs with mustard and relish baked potato chips apple sauce	fusilli pasta salad with zucchini, olives and sun-dried tomatoes	broiled halibut potato puffs salad	chicken steak on a roll with mushroom tomato sauce	Beef Fajitas [20] pineapple cubes

	MONDAY	TUESDAY	WEDNESDAY	THURSDAY	FRIDAY	SATURDAY	SUNDAY
BREAKFAST							
LUNCH							
SNACK							
DINNER							
QUICK DINNER							

	MONDAY	TUESDAY	WEDNESDAY	THURSDAY	FRIDAY	SATURDAY	SUNDAY
BREAKFAST	whole-grain cold cereal with raisins half grapefruit	scrambled eggs whole-grain toast sliced mango	Baked Apple [5] topped with yogurt and drizzled with honey and walnuts	multi-grain hot cereal topped with sliced bananas and sprinkled with cinnamon	grilled cheese and tomato cantaloupe cubes	veggie egg white omelette hash browns papaya cubes	blueberry pancakes with powdered sugar
LUNCH	Pear wedges spread with peanut butter celery sticks with ranch dressing	cream cheese and jam tea sandwiches pineapple chunks	turkey breast and cheddar cheese on a bagel with Dijon mustard clementine	egg salad in a pita with cucumber and tomato	cottage cheese with shredded carrots spread on bagel chips tangelo	green salad topped with sliced smoked turkey	baked potato topped with cheddar cheese and broccoli
SNACK	grapes	sliced banana and mandarin orange salad	oatmeal raisin cookie grapes	graham crackers glass of milk	cold veggies with salsa	popcorn warm apple cider	veggie sticks and pita chips with hummus
DINNER	chicken marsala orzo pasta salad	sauteed scallops over rice with mushrooms	broiled sirloin steak mashed potatoes sugar snap peas	Crispy Dijon Chicken [17] brown rice steamed broccoli	Teriyaki Grilled Salmon [27] rosemary new potatoes steamed green beans	manicotti with tomato sauce sauteed escarole in garlic and olive oil Italian bread	Squash and Chard Chili [22] warm corn muffins
QUICK DINNER	sauteed chicken cutlet with sun-dried tomatoes on focaccia bread salad	spring mix salad topped with sauteed scallops	hamburger on a whole wheat bun with lettuce and tomato strawberry apple sauce	Turkey Meatball Sub [19]	Fresh Tuna Burger [24] on a sesame seed bun with tartar sauce coleslaw	capellini pasta with pesto sauce Italian bread salad	Make Your Own Pizza: veggie pepperoni

	MONDAY	TUESDAY	WEDNESDAY	THURSDAY	FRIDAY	SATURDAY	SUNDAY
BREAKFAST							
LUNCH							
SNACK							
DINNER							
QUICK DINNER							

	MONDAY	TUESDAY	WEDNESDAY	THURSDAY	FRIDAY	SATURDAY	SUNDAY
BREAKFAST	Hole in One Eggs 8 half grapefruit	whole-grain waffles topped with almond butter and sliced bananas	cottage cheese topped with pineapple cubes and grapes	whole-grain cold cereal with sliced strawberries	warm cream of wheat with soy milk and raisins	grapefruit and orange sections topped with yogurt and wheat germ	cinnamon raisin French toast topped with sliced pears and maple syrup
LUNCH	pasta and bean soup whole-grain roll	turkey bologna on sourdough bread with lettuce and grainy mustard pear	tuna hoagie	hard-boiled egg whole-grain bagel with apple butter	peanut butter and banana slices on whole-grain bread	wagon wheel pasta with cubed ham, peas and diced tomatoes	French onion soup with melted cheese salad
SNACK	celery stuffed with cream cheese, topped with pecans	mango and kiwi slices	apple wedges dipped in honey	broccoli and cauliflower florets with warm melted cheese dip	pear and brie wedges	hot chocolate with whipped cream	cold veggies with vegetable-yogurt dip 1
DINNER	chicken Parmesan penne pasta sauteed broccoli rabe	broiled flank steak rice pilaf snow pea pods	Spinach Salad with Shrimp 27 rye crackers	sauteed turkey cutlets with onions, mushrooms, and red and green peppers	grilled salmon with mustard glaze Roasted Root Vegetables 30	lamb stew kasha and bowties	barbecued chicken potato salad coleslaw 28
QUICK DINNER	chicken quesadilla with sour cream and salsa	beef nachos	linguini with clam sauce raw baby carrots	turkey club sandwich on peasant bread	shrimp cocktail lettuce wedge with chopped tomato and blue cheese dressing	sloppy joe on a sesame seed bun raw baby carrots	Chicken and Artichokes 16 on sourdough bread

	MONDAY	TUESDAY	WEDNESDAY	THURSDAY	FRIDAY	SATURDAY	SUNDAY
BREAKFAST							
LUNCH							
SNACK							
DINNER							
QUICK DINNER							

	MONDAY	TUESDAY	WEDNESDAY	THURSDAY	FRIDAY	SATURDAY	SUNDAY
BREAKFAST	oatmeal with chopped apples and brown sugar	lemon scones with raspberry jam sliced pear	whole-grain cold cereal with sliced bananas and soy milk	orange sections and mango cubes topped with cottage cheese bran muffin	French toast sprinkled with powdered sugar pineapple chunks	warm millet cereal topped with chopped dates and pecans	buttermilk pancakes sliced strawberries
LUNCH	sliced Muenster cheese with sliced baby gherkins on pumpernickel bread raisins	lean ham and cheddar on a country biscuit grapes	seafood salad in a halved tomato celery sticks	sliced turkey and Swiss cheese on rye bread with whole-grain mustard cantaloupe wedge	hummus wrap with cucumber and tomato	egg salad on crostini crackers grape tomatoes	smoked salmon and herbed cream cheese tea sandwiches orange slices
SNACK	apple sauce sprinkled with cinnamon	cold veggies with low-fat sour cream and onion dip	peanut butter and jam on whole-grain crackers half grapefruit	oatmeal raisin cookie glass of milk	rice pudding warm apple cider	zucchini muffins [11]	pear wedges dipped in vanilla yogurt topped with slivered almonds
DINNER	beef stuffed peppers salad	Turkey Meatloaf [19] rice pilaf cucumber and corn salad	Mac and Cheese [13] steamed broccoli	vegetarian chili warm corn bread salad	grilled tuna sautéed zucchini, onions and new potatoes salad	chicken cacciatore angel hair pasta steamed mustard greens	filet of beef butternut squash sautéed green beans
QUICK DINNER	country beef vegetable soup warm popovers	Zippy Turkey Pesto [19] corn salad	Pasta with sautéed fresh spinach garlic toast kiwi slices	grilled fresh mozzarella, roasted red pepper and avocado sandwich on whole-grain bread	Make Your Own Pizza: shrimp and veggie pizza	Chicken Fajitas [16] with green peppers and onions	minute steak sandwich on a long roll topped with sautéed mushrooms and tomato sauce

	MONDAY	TUESDAY	WEDNESDAY	THURSDAY	FRIDAY	SATURDAY	SUNDAY
BREAKFAST							
LUNCH							
SNACK							
DINNER							
QUICK DINNER							

	MONDAY	TUESDAY	WEDNESDAY	THURSDAY	FRIDAY	SATURDAY	SUNDAY
BREAKFAST	oatmeal topped with berries and sprinkled with cinnamon sugar	fruit and yogurt smoothie whole-grain toast	challah toast spread with almond butter and topped with sliced bananas	hard-boiled egg raisin toast with apricot jam	whole-grain cold cereal with sliced strawberries	buckwheat pancakes with honey fresh figs	bagel topped with cream cheese and smoked salmon pineapple chunks
LUNCH	tuna salad with diced apples on raisin bread	turkey bologna on rye bread with yellow mustard broccoli florets dipped in ranch dressing	lean ham roll-ups melba toast grapes	sliced turkey wrapped around carrot sticks dipped in honey mustard	fruit kabob cheddar cheese wedge sesame crackers	peanut butter and pumpkin butter on toast apple wedges	Cold Pea Soup [3] salad
SNACK	whole-grain crackers low-sodium vegetable juice	tortilla chips sprinkled with Monterey Jack cheese, broiled or microwaved salsa	orange wedges	Italian bread slices dipped in marinara sauce	cold veggies with hummus	frozen grapes	yogurt topped with sliced kiwi and raspberries
DINNER	vegetable Puff with Asiago Cheese [11]	broiled filet of sole wheat berries steamed green beans	Chicken Fajitas [16] with sour cream and guacamole	wagon wheel pasta topped with sautéed shiitake mushrooms and snow peas in garlic olive oil Italian bread	beef chili warm corn bread cucumber and corn salad	veal roast rosemary garlic new potatoes Honey-Ginger Carrots [29]	eggplant Parmesan angel hair pasta
QUICK DINNER	asparagus, brie and roasted red pepper omelette	Oven-Baked Fried Fish [25] Potato Puffs radishes	turkey melt Pear	spaghetti with red or white clam sauce garlic cheese toast salad	hot deli roast beef sandwich with gravy instant mashed potatoes apple sauce	chopped chef's salad with raw veggies	veggie hot dogs baked beans baby carrots

	MONDAY	TUESDAY	WEDNESDAY	THURSDAY	FRIDAY	SATURDAY	SUNDAY
BREAKFAST							
LUNCH							
SNACK							
DINNER							
QUICK DINNER							

	MONDAY	TUESDAY	WEDNESDAY	THURSDAY	FRIDAY	SATURDAY	SUNDAY
BREAKFAST	whole-grain cold cereal topped with fresh raspberries and soy milk	warm millet cereal with fresh blueberries and slivered almonds	whole-grain waffle with peach butter honeydew melon wedge	Banana Nut Bread 5 spread with walnut butter	cottage cheese topped with blackberries and sprinkled with crunchy granola	scrambled eggs on whole-grain toast with melted soy cheese half grapefruit	Cheese Blintzes 7 with cherry topping
LUNCH	roast beef hoagie celery sticks	cubed ham, cheese, and fruit kabob pumpernickel roll	cold elbow pasta with cheddar cheese cubes and olives grapes	seafood salad on a croissant with lettuce and tomato strawberries	turkey on whole wheat bread with lettuce and grainy mustard carrot sticks	pita wedges and raw veggies dipped in baba ghanoush	cashew butter spread on a cinnamon raisin bagel cantaloupe cubes
SNACK	Lemon-Poppy Seed Loaf 9 sliced orange	zucchini, cucumber and red peppers salsa	apple wedges dipped in honey	whole edamame (frozen soybeans) veggie juice	celery sticks and cauliflower with Spinach Dip 1	chilled strawberry soup	broiled pineapple skewers
DINNER	fettuccini with chicken and pine nuts salad	seafood chowder crusty bread fruit salad	broiled or grilled sirloin steak baked potato steamed green beans	roast turkey breast, stuffing and gravy Steamed Brussels Sprouts 30 cranberry relish	vegetable pot pie salad	spaghetti with Tiny Meatballs 23 salad Italian bread	grilled salmon oven-roasted new potatoes and asparagus broiled tomato halves
QUICK DINNER	pasta with sauteed spinach and tomatoes	sauteed bay scallops in garlic butter served over spring mix dinner rolls	beef or turkey burgers on a whole-grain bun oven fries coleslaw	chicken, snow peas and cashew stir-fry quick brown rice	bean tacos shredded cheese, shredded lettuce and olives	turkey bacon, lettuce and tomato sandwich	vegetable omelette microwaved Baked Apples 9

	MONDAY	TUESDAY	WEDNESDAY	THURSDAY	FRIDAY	SATURDAY	SUNDAY
BREAKFAST							
LUNCH							
SNACK							
DINNER							
QUICK DINNER							

	MONDAY	TUESDAY	WEDNESDAY	THURSDAY	FRIDAY	SATURDAY	SUNDAY
BREAKFAST	mixed berry and yogurt smoothie toasted pita	Pizza bagel	whole-grain cold cereal with raisins orange wedges	mango slices topped with raspberries and plain yogurt, drizzled with orange blossom honey	grilled white cheddar cheese with tomato and veggie bacon on sourdough	Puffed Pancake 10 turkey sausage sliced bananas	challah French toast topped with sliced strawberries and cinnamon sugar
LUNCH	beef salami and Swiss cheese cubes dipped in honey mustard Pear	almond butter spread on apple slices topped with raisins	egg salad on pumpernickel with lettuce and tomato	smoked turkey and Muenster cheese on rye bread with grainy mustard apple sauce	garden salad topped with turkey breast slices	vegetable soup hummus and pita triangles	vegetable sushi miso soup
SNACK	cold veggies with thousand island dressing	frozen banana slices	warm apple cider oatmeal cookie	celery stuffed with cream cheese	popcorn sprinkled with chili powder	apple	Peanut butter and jam on whole-grain crackers dried apricots
DINNER	barbecued chicken and pineapple kabob basmati rice salad	broiled flounder crispy oven-baked fries Coleslaw 28	veal piccata buttered noodles sauteed spinach in olive oil	Couscous Salad with Beans and Greens 12 endive, watercress and walnut salad	Quick and Easy Ratatouille 29 sauteed potatoes salad	Mac and Cheese 13 with ham and peas stewed tomatoes	chicken Parmesan on a roll Caesar salad
QUICK DINNER	Zippy Turkey Pesto 19 carrot and celery sticks	shrimp salad stuffed tomato blackberries	Potato and cheese pierogies steamed broccoli garlic toast	Turkey (or beef) Enchilada 19 avocado and tomato salad	garden veggie burger with lettuce and tomato grapes	Pasta with Tomatoes and Olives 14 Italian bread	sauteed chicken breasts minute rice cucumber slices

	MONDAY	TUESDAY	WEDNESDAY	THURSDAY	FRIDAY	SATURDAY	SUNDAY
BREAKFAST							
LUNCH							
SNACK							
DINNER							
QUICK DINNER							

	MONDAY	TUESDAY	WEDNESDAY	THURSDAY	FRIDAY	SATURDAY	SUNDAY
BREAKFAST	vanilla yogurt topped with granola and fresh raspberries	Hole in One Eggs 8 half grapefruit	raisin toast with sliced apple and melted soy cheese	oatmeal topped with chopped dates and sprinkled with brown sugar	cold whole-grain cereal with sliced bananas	pineapple chunks, orange and grapefruit sections topped with cottage cheese and pecans	cornmeal waffles drizzled with honey strawberries
LUNCH	ham and herbed cream cheese wrap cantaloupe wedge	tuna salad on Italian roll with lettuce and tomato	roast beef on peasant bread with horseradish sauce orange wedges	veggie turkey and soy cheese on whole-grain crackers with grainy mustard grapes	bagel chips with Spinach Dip 1 apple	chicken vegetable soup whole-grain crackers	grilled brie and Dijon mustard on French bread grapes
SNACK	Zucchini muffins 11 a handful of raisins	cold veggies with Cucumber Dip 1	minestrone soup oyster crackers	a handful of pistachios tomato juice	banana slices dipped in wheat germ	roasted eggplant spread on crostini crackers grapes	carrot and celery sticks with onion dip
DINNER	Salmon with Red Onions 26 creamed spinach salad	Chicken and Artichokes 16 Parsleyed new potatoes salad	farfalle pasta with asparagus tips sliced tomatoes with fresh basil	vegetarian chili warm corn bread salad	Light Crab Cakes 24 served over mixed green salad with cocktail sauce	Teriyaki London Broil 23 Carrot Souffle 28 sugar snap peas	chicken pot pie garden salad
QUICK DINNER	baked potato with grated cheese and mixed veggies	tofu dog on a roll with sauerkraut and relish	spinach and cheese ravioli with melted butter and pine nuts	Baked Burritos 12 with shredded cheese, olives and sour cream salad	Poached eggs on rye toast veggie bacon grapefruit sections	hot deli roast beef sandwich with gravy apple sauce	chicken salad over mixed greens

	MONDAY	TUESDAY	WEDNESDAY	THURSDAY	FRIDAY	SATURDAY	SUNDAY
BREAKFAST							
LUNCH							
SNACK							
DINNER							
QUICK DINNER							

	MONDAY	TUESDAY	WEDNESDAY	THURSDAY	FRIDAY	SATURDAY	SUNDAY
BREAKFAST	fried eggs toasted whole wheat pita orange slices	mutli-grain hot cereal with diced pears and soy milk	Banana Nut Bread 5 spread with Peach butter	whole-grain waffle with maple syrup sliced bananas	fruit and yogurt smoothie	bagel topped with cream cheese and smoked salmon pineapple and kiwi chunks	mixed berries topped with yogurt and a crumbled bran muffin
LUNCH	papaya and mango kabob string cheese whole-grain crackers	almond butter and fruit preserves on graham crackers zucchini sticks	veggie pepperoni and soy cheese kabob Pear	tuna salad with diced apples on raisin bread with lettuce	egg salad on peasant bread with cucumber slices and red pepper rings	grilled pepper Jack cheese on rye with roasted peppers	tomato soup turkey wrapped around carrot sticks oyster crackers
SNACK	tortilla chips with guacamole and salsa	strawberries dipped in vanilla yogurt and rolled in brown sugar	frozen grapes	cold veggies and hummus	fresh dates	oatmeal cookie fresh grapefruit juice	Pumpernickel rounds with White Bean Dip 2
DINNER	swordfish with chopped tomatoes and capers wild rice sauteed spinach	fried chicken baked potato wedges steamed sugar snap peas	Pasta Frittata 9 cucumber and tomato salad	grilled veal chops Broccoli in Creamy Balsamic Sauce 28 Honey-Ginger Carrots 29	roast chicken roasted potatoes with thyme steamed green beans salad	vegetable stir-fry brown rice with raisins and cashews	rack of lamb buttered baby turnips Roasted Asparagus with Cheese and Pine Nuts 29
QUICK DINNER	shrimp cocktail sliced tomatoes with balsamic vinaigrette coleslaw	sauteed turkey cutlets topped with sun-dried tomatoes and mushrooms on sourdough bread	rigatoni with black and green olives Italian bread	sloppy joe on a whole-grain bun carrot and celery sticks with ranch dressing	Chicken Fajitas 16 with green peppers and onions cantaloupe and honeydew cubes	Pasta with butter and Parmesan cheese garden salad	Make Your Own Pizza: Mexican 13

	MONDAY	TUESDAY	WEDNESDAY	THURSDAY	FRIDAY	SATURDAY	SUNDAY
BREAKFAST							
LUNCH							
SNACK							
DINNER							
QUICK DINNER							

	MONDAY	TUESDAY	WEDNESDAY	THURSDAY	FRIDAY	SATURDAY	SUNDAY
BREAKFAST	mango, blueberry and star fruit salad sprinkled with walnuts	scrambled eggs on a bagel with melted soy cheese half grapefruit	grilled peanut butter and jam sandwich	cantaloupe wedge with a scoop of cottage cheese rye toast	English muffin pizza	lean ham slices on crusty French bread strawberries	blueberry blintzes with low-fat sour cream
LUNCH	chicken salad on a croissant with lettuce red grapes	apple wedges spread with almond butter and sprinkled with granola	tuna salad hoagie with lettuce and tomato	black bean soup chopped veggie salad	turkey, honeydew and strawberry kabob rice cakes	pasta salad with flaked tuna, broccoli and olives	roast beef on a whole-grain roll with spicy mustard grapes
SNACK	cold veggies with Asparagus Dip [1]	Pumpkin Muffins [10] mandarin oranges	pineapple and honeydew cubes dipped in yogurt	a handful of pecans vegetable juice	sesame breadsticks dipped in whipped cream cheese	baked pears with cinnamon	banana
DINNER	Linguini with Shrimp Scampi [25] salad	Fast and Easy Chicken Chili [17] corn bread salad	Homemade Fried Rice [13] salad with ginger dressing	meatloaf mashed potatoes peas natural apple sauce	grilled red snapper couscous sautéed onions and summer squash	barbecued chicken baked beans Coleslaw [28]	Tomato-Spinach Risotto [15] salad
QUICK DINNER	sautéed shrimp in olive oil with spinach toasted onion roll	turkey and brie on honey-wheat bread with lettuce and mustard kiwi slices	orzo pasta with roasted red peppers and black olives	turkey or beef burgers oven fries raw baby carrots	scallop stir-fry couscous lettuce wedge	deviled eggs salad topped with chopped apple and sunflower seeds	grilled Muenster cheese with sliced gherkins on pumpernickel bread with grainy mustard orange

	MONDAY	TUESDAY	WEDNESDAY	THURSDAY	FRIDAY	SATURDAY	SUNDAY
BREAKFAST							
LUNCH							
SNACK							
DINNER							
QUICK DINNER							

SPRING

	BREAKFAST	LUNCH	SNACK	DINNER	QUICK DINNER
MONDAY	poached eggs on whole-grain toast, half grapefruit	veggie pepperoni and cheese slices on whole-grain crackers, honeydew wedge	frozen grapes	grilled tuna, wild rice, sautéed carrots	tuna salad mixed with great northern beans on a bed of lettuce
TUESDAY	plain yogurt topped with raspberries and sprinkled with granola, whole-grain cold cereal with sliced bananas	seafood salad on a bagel with lettuce and tomato, sesame crackers	whole edamame (frozen soybeans), veggie juice	roast turkey, roasted potatoes, broccoli au gratin	deli turkey, cream cheese and salsa wrap
WEDNESDAY	whole-grain cold cereal with sliced bananas	egg salad in a halved tomato, sesame crackers	cold veggies and hummus	pasta with steamed asparagus tips and goat cheese, garlic toast	elbow noodles topped with crumbled goat cheese and sun-dried tomatoes
THURSDAY	sliced pear on raisin bread with melted soy cheese	lean ham roll-ups, whole-grain crackers, apple	vanilla yogurt topped with sliced strawberries	veal marsala, buttered noodles, fresh peas	tofu and vegetable stir-fry
FRIDAY	millet hot cereal with blueberries	peanut butter and banana on whole-grain crackers, apple	pineapple chunks	sole almondine, corn nibblets, creamed spinach	Make Your Own Pizza: mild and wild fresh tomatoes and mushrooms
SATURDAY	blackberry and banana smoothie	smoked salmon and herbed cream cheese tea sandwiches, kiwi slices	popcorn, vegetable sticks	chicken Parmesan, angel hair pasta, sautéed zucchini and tomatoes	chicken quesadilla with salsa and sour cream
SUNDAY	egg white omelette with sautéed veggies, orange wedges	vegetable soup, rye crackers	apple sauce sprinkled with nutmeg	filet of beef, Spaghetti Squash Sauté 30, sautéed green beans	Pierogies Primavera 15

	MONDAY	TUESDAY	WEDNESDAY	THURSDAY	FRIDAY	SATURDAY	SUNDAY
BREAKFAST							
LUNCH							
SNACK							
DINNER							
QUICK DINNER							

	BREAKFAST	LUNCH	SNACK	DINNER	QUICK DINNER
MONDAY	whole-grain cold cereal with sliced bananas and soy milk	cream cheese and fruit jam on whole wheat bread	frozen mini egg rolls	sauteed scallops served over rice with sauteed spinach	seafood chowder / crusty bread / salad
TUESDAY	orange sections and strawberries topped with yogurt and a crumbled blueberry muffin	tuna salad on an onion roll with lettuce and shredded carrots	apple wedges with brie	roasted turkey breast / creamed corn / broccoli with cashews / salad	Turkey Enchilada 19
WEDNESDAY	whole-grain waffle with almond butter and raisins	egg salad and cucumber slices on a bagel	carrot sticks with veggie Dip 2	baked potato with cheddar cheese / salad	sauteed vegetables on French bread
THURSDAY	Zucchini Bread 11 spread with peach butter	ham, cheddar cheese and honeydew cube kabob / whole-grain crackers	oat bran muffin	Vegetable Lasagna 15 / crusty bread / salad	mushroom ravioli with tomato sauce / peas
FRIDAY	oatmeal sprinkled with cinnamon sugar and fresh berries	sliced turkey and mozzarella on whole-grain bread with lettuce, tomato and brown mustard	tortilla chips and salsa	Italian Tuna, White Bean and Escarole Salad 24 / salad	Shrimp and White Bean Salad 26 / raw baby carrots
SATURDAY	French toast topped with sauteed bananas	sushi / green salad with ginger dressing	pineapple chunks dipped in melted chocolate	marinated flank steak / Spaghetti Squash Saute 30 / oven-roasted asparagus	tacos / shredded cheese, shredded lettuce, and olives
SUNDAY	mango slices topped with cottage cheese	Pasta e Fagioli soup / Italian bread	strawberries	Lemon Chicken 17 / Roasted Root Vegetables 30 / salad	sauteed chicken tenders on focaccia bread with pesto sauce

QUICK DINNER

DINNER

SNACK

LUNCH

BREAKFAST

MONDAY

TUESDAY

WEDNESDAY

THURSDAY

FRIDAY

SATURDAY

SUNDAY

	MONDAY	TUESDAY	WEDNESDAY	THURSDAY	FRIDAY	SATURDAY	SUNDAY
BREAKFAST	warm millet cereal topped with blueberries	sliced Pears with Maple Yogurt 9	scrambled eggs with fresh herbs toasted bagel half grapefruit	grilled cheese with lean ham and tomato	pizza bagel	Puffed Pancake 10 melon wedge	cold cereal with sliced bananas and soy milk
LUNCH	beef salami on rye bread with yellow mustard orange sections	almond butter, fruit jam and granola wrap celery sticks	crusty French bread and a wedge of fontina cheese grapes	turkey salad on pumpernickel bread	garden salad topped with flaked tuna whole-grain roll	hummus and tabbouleh in pita with tomato	turkey and cheese roll-ups coleslaw
SNACK	cheese biscuit apple wedges	jicama and cucumber sticks with White Bean Dip 2	a handful of nuts, sunflower seeds and dried cranberries	cold veggies with ranch dip	frozen banana slices	cottage cheese topped with blackberries	cauliflower florets dipped in thousand island dressing
DINNER	vegetable Puff with Asiago Cheese 11 salad	Crispy Dijon Chicken 17 roasted red bliss potatoes carrot raisin salad	veal roast wild rice sugar snap peas	mushroom risotto tomato and onion salad garlic bread	Fast and Easy Chicken Chili 17 warm corn bread salad	Panzanella with White Beans and Goat Cheese 14	cold strawberry soup Teriyaki Grilled Salmon 27 barley green beans
QUICK DINNER	Poached eggs, soy Canadian bacon and melted cheese on a toasted English muffin	teriyaki turkey burger lettuce wedge carrots, olives and pickles	hot deli roast beef sandwich with gravy instant mashed potatoes steamed carrots	capellini pasta with peas, pine nuts and chopped tomatoes	sauteed chicken cutlets with escarole on toasted Italian bread	Baked Burritos 12 with corn and tomato salsa	Pierogies Pesto 14 apple

	QUICK DINNER	DINNER	SNACK	LUNCH	BREAKFAST
MONDAY					
TUESDAY					
WEDNESDAY					
THURSDAY					
FRIDAY					
SATURDAY					
SUNDAY					

	MONDAY	TUESDAY	WEDNESDAY	THURSDAY	FRIDAY	SATURDAY	SUNDAY
BREAKFAST	strawberries dipped in plain yogurt and rolled in wheat germ	oatmeal with soy milk topped with blackberries	cantaloupe and honeydew cubes topped with a scoop of cottage cheese	Hole in One Eggs 8 orange wedges	whole-grain waffle with almond butter and sliced bananas	fruit smoothie bran muffin	Cheese Blintzes 7 topped with cherry sauce
LUNCH	corkscrew pasta with cubes of cheese zucchini sticks	celery stuffed with peanut butter rolled in chopped dates	chicken rice soup whole-grain crackers raw baby carrots	garden salad topped with sliced smoked turkey and sun-dried tomatoes	ham and cheese hoagie	turkey breast on rye bread with coleslaw and Russian dressing	egg salad in a whole wheat pita with tomato and sprouts
SNACK	figs	cream cheese and grated carrots on cinnamon raisin bread	sliced red and orange peppers with onion dip	pear	bagel chips with herbed cream cheese celery sticks	cold veggies and hummus	vegetable juice whole-grain bread sticks
DINNER	Light Crab Cakes 24 sauteed potatoes and onions steamed green beans	Pineapple chicken herbed couscous tomato and cucumber salad	quiche Lorraine spring mix salad	Potato gnocchi topped with steamed veggies salad	shrimp scampi basmati rice with cashews tomato and mozzarella salad	rack of lamb Carrot Souffle 28 steamed asparagus	tofu and mixed veggie stir-fry brown rice salad
QUICK DINNER	crabmeat over spring-mix with cocktail sauce oven-fries	chicken tacos shredded cheese, lettuce and tomato sandwich sour cream	turkey bacon, lettuce and tomato sandwich	Potato gnocchi topped with marinara sauce salad	Shrimp Wrap with Corn Salsa 26	minute steak sandwiches with sauteed onions and peppers on a crusty roll	Roasted Potatoes Topped with Sun-Dried Tomato Pesto 30 salad half grapefruit

QUICK DINNER

DINNER

SNACK

LUNCH

BREAKFAST

MONDAY

TUESDAY

WEDNESDAY

THURSDAY

FRIDAY

SATURDAY

SUNDAY

	MONDAY	TUESDAY	WEDNESDAY	THURSDAY	FRIDAY	SATURDAY	SUNDAY
BREAKFAST	whole-grain cold cereal with sliced strawberries	whole-grain waffle with maple syrup banana	cinnamon raisin bagel with soy cream cheese and raspberry jam	grilled peanut butter and jam sandwich	warm cream of wheat with a swirl of honey half grapefruit	plain yogurt topped with sliced kiwi and mangoes	French toast topped with fresh strawberries, sprinkled with powdered sugar
LUNCH	cashew butter and apricot jam on a multi-grain roll	tomato soup wedge of cheddar cheese apple	seafood salad on crostini crackers cucumber spears	sliced turkey breast wrapped around carrot sticks	tuna salad on a kaiser roll with lettuce and tomato	turkey bologna on rye toast with lettuce, tomato and yellow mustard	chopped garden salad with raw veggies
SNACK	Italian bread dipped in marinara sauce	watermelon cubes	fresh apricot	edamame (frozen soybeans) veggie juice	cold veggies and salsa	popcorn sprinkled with grated cheese grapes	oatmeal raisin cookie glass of milk
DINNER	grilled halibut orzo pasta with stewed tomatoes sauteed spinach	Chicken Fajitas 16 with onions and green peppers Spanish rice	Far Eastern Steak Salad 21 Pineapple chunks	Vegetable Lasagna 15 orange sections	Baked Breaded Chicken 16 shoestring potatoes sauteed broccoli with mushrooms	egg white omelette with Quick and Easy Ratatouille 29	salmon cakes kasha Honey-Ginger Carrots 29
QUICK DINNER	sauteed scallops over spinach salad	hot deli turkey sandwich with gravy steamed carrots	beef stir-fry salad	Pasta with Artichoke Hearts and Feta Cheese 14 garlic bread	Turkey Meatball Sub 19	garden salad topped with a scoop of egg salad carrot and celery sticks	Make Your Own Pizza: ground beef Microwaved Baked Apples 9

	MONDAY	TUESDAY	WEDNESDAY	THURSDAY	FRIDAY	SATURDAY	SUNDAY
BREAKFAST							
LUNCH							
SNACK							
DINNER							
QUICK DINNER							

	MONDAY	TUESDAY	WEDNESDAY	THURSDAY	FRIDAY	SATURDAY	SUNDAY
BREAKFAST	raisin toast with sliced pears and melted soy cheese	banana berry smoothie biscotti	Breakfast Fajita 5 watermelon cubes	cantaloupe with fruit salsa	cold whole-grain cereal topped with blueberries	buckwheat pancakes topped with raspberries and drizzled with honey half grapefruit	fried egg whites turkey sausage honeydew wedge
LUNCH	apple wedges spread with peanut butter and topped with raisins graham crackers	sliced turkey breast and provolone cheese on French bread with arugula and mustard-mayonnaise dressing	tuna salad with sliced cherry tomatoes vegetable soup	pepper Jack cheese and roasted peppers on focaccia bread	cubed turkey, grape and pineapple kabob	roast beef roll-ups sesame crackers grapes	grilled cheddar cheese with tomato on sourdough bread
SNACK	cold veggies and ranch dressing	mini pizza bagels	jicama and cucumber sticks	pita wedges with roasted eggplant dip	whole-grain crackers with fruit jam	Banana Nut Bread 5 spread with peach butter	onion soup with croutons carrot and celery sticks
DINNER	chicken scallopini wild mushroom risotto salad	penne pasta with crabmeat and spinach	vegetarian chili warm corn bread	corned beef, cabbage and potatoes	Cold Pea Soup 3 steamed red snapper filet Jasmine rice	Pasta Chicken Caesar Salad 18 Italian bread orange slices	tofu and vegetable stir-fry salad with ginger dressing
QUICK DINNER	chicken cutlet Parmesan on a roll	Mac and Cheese 13 stewed tomatoes	quick brown rice with chopped tomatoes, olives and cannelini beans	lean corned beef Reuben sandwich	shrimp cocktail Roasted Asparagus with Cheese and Pine Nuts 29	sliced rotisserie chicken sandwich orange slices	tofu hot dog on a roll with mustard and relish sliced tomatoes

	BREAKFAST	LUNCH	SNACK	DINNER	QUICK DINNER
MONDAY					
TUESDAY					
WEDNESDAY					
THURSDAY					
FRIDAY					
SATURDAY					
SUNDAY					

	MONDAY	TUESDAY	WEDNESDAY	THURSDAY	FRIDAY	SATURDAY	SUNDAY
BREAKFAST	yogurt topped with crushed pineapple and strawberries	whole-grain cold cereal with soy milk and sliced bananas	toasted whole wheat English muffin spread with almond butter and fruit jam	hot millet cereal topped with blueberries	whole-grain pancakes with apricot jam	apple blintzes topped with low-fat sour cream	smoked salmon and herbed cream cheese tea sandwiches honeydew wedge
LUNCH	beef salami cubes dipped in honey mustard breadsticks apple	cream cheese and grated carrots on cinnamon raisin bread	egg salad on pumpernickel bread with shredded lettuce	turkey club sandwich mandarin oranges	vegetable barley soup whole-grain crackers with gouda cheese	pita stuffed with hummus, sprouts and sliced tomatoes	Caesar salad with sliced chicken
SNACK	crusty French bread topped with a wedge of brie grapes	fresh berries	cold veggies and Asparagus Dip 1	mini carrot muffins 6 with fruit jam	a handful of pecans and raisins	half grapefruit	graham crackers and marshmallows dipped in melted chocolate
DINNER	mahi-mahi with pine nuts buttered new potatoes roasted fresh beets	chicken florentine basmati rice salad	manicotti with mushroom tomato sauce salad	Osso Buco 21 roasted potatoes salad	grilled tuna bulgar wheat steamed green beans	barbecued chicken corn fritters cucumber and tomato salad	asparagus and Swiss cheese omelette sliced orange and black olive salad
QUICK DINNER	scallops with almonds 26 salad	chicken quesadilla salsa sour cream	angel hair pasta with black olives, capers and crumbled goat cheese pear	Beef Fajitas 20	Spinach Salad with Shrimp 27	grilled cheese with sliced turkey breast on whole-grain bread apple sauce	jelly omelette toasted bagel fresh apricot

QUICK DINNER

DINNER

SNACK

LUNCH

BREAKFAST

MONDAY

TUESDAY

WEDNESDAY

THURSDAY

FRIDAY

SATURDAY

SUNDAY

	MONDAY	TUESDAY	WEDNESDAY	THURSDAY	FRIDAY	SATURDAY	SUNDAY
BREAKFAST	raisin toast spread with peanut butter and topped with sliced bananas	Zucchini Bread [11] spread with peach butter	cold multi-grain cereal topped with blueberries	hard-boiled egg / wedge of soy cheese / mixed berries	toasted bagel with cream cheese and fruit jam	oatmeal sprinkled with brown sugar, cinnamon and raisins	Western omelette topped with salsa
LUNCH	turkey bologna wrapped around a cheese stick dipped in honey mustard / apple sauce	roast beef on an onion roll with horseradish sauce	tuna salad on five-grain bread with shredded lettuce	almond butter stuffed celery sticks rolled in raisins	smoked turkey, sliced fresh mozzarella on a French baguette with spicy mustard and pickles	Baked Burritos [12] / apple wedges	Peach and nectarine slices topped with yogurt and chopped walnuts
SNACK	cold veggies and Spinach Dip [1]	frozen grapes / Pineapple chunks	watermelon wedge	plum	orange	cherries	mini blueberry muffins
DINNER	Light Crab Cakes [24] / sliced tomatoes with basil / Potato salad	apricot chicken / Jasmine rice / steamed green beans	eggplant Parmesan / Italian bread / salad	grilled flank steak / buttered noodles / grilled zucchini	chilled Gazpacho [3] / broiled tilapia / Roasted Asparagus with Cheese and Pine Nuts [29]	Tomato-Spinach Risotto [15] / salad / Papaya and star fruit slices	Baked Breaded Chicken [16] / corn on the cob / steamed broccoli
QUICK DINNER	Caesar salad topped with lump crabmeat / mango cubes and raspberries	sesame chicken tenders / snow pea pods / salad	Make Your Own Pizza: Primavera [13]	Zesty Barbecue Pitas [23] / salad	Shrimp and White Bean Salad [26]	capellini with sautéed bay scallops and peas / salad	sautéed chicken and escarole

QUICK DINNER

DINNER

SNACK

LUNCH

BREAKFAST

MONDAY

TUESDAY

WEDNESDAY

THURSDAY

FRIDAY

SATURDAY

SUNDAY

	BREAKFAST	LUNCH	SNACK	DINNER	QUICK DINNER
MONDAY	fruit smoothie / Banana Nut Muffin 5	sliced lean ham on a country biscuit with grainy mustard / granny smith apple	peach	brook trout with sauteed onions and almonds / rice pilaf / shredded sauteed zucchini	Fresh Tuna Burgers 24 on a whole-grain bun with lettuce and tomato / coleslaw
TUESDAY	Hole in One eggs 8 / half grapefruit	tossed garden salad topped with turkey and cheese cubes	cold veggies with salsa / glass of milk	veal roast / browned paprika potatoes / cauliflower with cheese sauce	veal piccata / angel hair pasta
WEDNESDAY	cold whole-grain cereal with sliced strawberries	cream cheese and grated carrots spread on cinnamon bread	oatmeal raisin cookie / glass of milk	chilled zucchini Soup 3 / romaine salad topped with sliced grilled chicken	chicken steak sandwich with tomato sauce and fried onions
THURSDAY	melted soy cheese on whole-grain bagel / cantaloupe wedge	tuna salad with diced apples and dried apricots on wheat bread	blackberries	ravioli topped with marinara sauce / hearts of palm salad / garlic bread	ravioli topped with melted butter and Parmesan cheese / nectarine
FRIDAY	sliced plums topped with yogurt and granola	egg salad on a whole-grain roll with sprouts / grapes	veggie sticks and blue corn chips with Hot Bean Dip 1	seafood stew / sauteed sugar snap peas / Italian bread	Salmon Baked in Foil 25 / gnocchi with melted butter / baby carrots
SATURDAY	peanut butter and raspberry Jam on whole-grain toast	Pasta Salad with raw veggies in a vinaigrette	frozen juice pop	barbecued chicken / parsleyed buttered rice / steamed green beans / salad	Chicken and Artichokes 16 / red pepper strips
SUNDAY	Cheddar Cornmeal Waffles 6 with maple syrup / blueberries	veggie pepperoni and soy cheese stuffed in a whole wheat pita with ranch dressing / banana	pineapple chunks and mandarin oranges	linguini with asparagus and goat cheese / salad / breadsticks	Pasta with Tomatoes and Olives 14 / bread sticks

	MONDAY	TUESDAY	WEDNESDAY	THURSDAY	FRIDAY	SATURDAY	SUNDAY
BREAKFAST							
LUNCH							
SNACK							
DINNER							
QUICK DINNER							

SUMMER

	MONDAY	TUESDAY	WEDNESDAY	THURSDAY	FRIDAY	SATURDAY	SUNDAY
BREAKFAST	whole-grain cold cereal with sliced bananas	Poached eggs and soy Canadian bacon on a whole wheat English muffin cantaloupe cubes	pizza bagel	turkey and cheese roll-ups cherries	fruit kabob dipped in vanilla yogurt	whole-grain pancakes sprinkled with raspberries and powdered sugar	egg white omelette whole-grain toast blueberries
LUNCH	Antipasto Salad 28 sourdough bread	apple wedges spread with almond butter topped with wheat germ	cream cheese and fruit jam wrap	seafood salad on a croissant with lettuce	garden salad topped with lean ham	Cold Pea Soup 3 cottage cheese topped with crushed pineapple	turkey bologna on rye toast with yellow mustard pear
SNACK	frozen grapes	graham crackers with peach butter	nectarine	Homemade Trail Mix 8 veggie juice	cold veggies with Cucumber Dip 1	whole-grain crackers with soy cheese sliced apple	banana slices dipped in granola
DINNER	filet roast sauteed mushrooms Roasted Asparagus with Cheese and Pine Nuts 29	Turkey Meatloaf 19 baked sweet potato fries steamed cabbage	baked monkfish in lemon butter couscous creamed spinach	Pasta Primavera Italian bread	roasted cornish game hen basmati rice sauteed mustard greens with garlic	grilled shrimp kabob corn on the cob grilled veggies	vegetable pot pie sliced plums
QUICK DINNER	Beef Fajitas 20 quick Spanish rice	Capered Chicken Cutlets 16 sugar snap peas multi-grain roll	crabmeat quesadillas	sauteed veggie hoagie	Turkey Enchilada 19 mixed berries	shrimp cocktail rosemary focaccia	veggie burger on a whole-grain bun with lettuce and tomato

	MONDAY	TUESDAY	WEDNESDAY	THURSDAY	FRIDAY	SATURDAY	SUNDAY
BREAKFAST							
LUNCH							
SNACK							
DINNER							
QUICK DINNER							

	MONDAY	TUESDAY	WEDNESDAY	THURSDAY	FRIDAY	SATURDAY	SUNDAY
BREAKFAST	sliced fresh peaches and apricots topped with cottage cheese and mixed berries oat bran muffin	cinnamon raisin bagel topped with soy cream cheese and orange marmalade	oatmeal topped with blackberries and sliced bananas	Blueberry Breakfast Shake 5 pumpernickel toast	whole-grain cold cereal with sliced peaches	challah French toast with maple syrup sliced orange	fresh figs and brie on a French baguette
LUNCH	garden salad topped with chickpeas and chopped veggies	chilled cantaloupe soup tortilla chips dipped in hummus	tuna salad with shredded carrots and golden raisins on whole-grain bread	Muenster cheese with sliced gherkins and grainy mustard on peasant bread pear	smoked turkey cobb salad	tabbouleh with diced tomatoes and cucumbers served with pita wedges	chilled Gazpacho 3 shrimp cocktail with mustard-mayo sauce
SNACK	frozen pineapple chunks	cheddar cheese wedge grapes	popcorn drizzled with herb olive oil	celery stuffed with peanut butter and chopped dates	mini egg rolls	cold veggies with Asparagus Dip 1	plain yogurt topped with dried cranberries
DINNER	paella orange and black olive salad	Far Eastern Steak Salad 21 honeydew	grilled vegetable kabob quinoa grilled pineapple slices	Mac and Cheese 13 steamed broccoli	Poached salmon with dill sauce cucumber and tomato salad crusty rolls	Teriyaki London Broil, 23 white rice with cashews, grilled cherry tomato and mushroom skewers	roasted turkey breast oven browned potatoes, carrots and onions lima beans
QUICK DINNER	elbow pasta with scallops, tomatoes and herbs	roast beef on rye bread with Russian dressing	tofu franks vegetarian baked beans coleslaw	scrambled eggs turkey sausage hash browns cherries	Manhattan clam chowder oyster crackers plum	beef tacos shredded lettuce, tomato and olives	sauteed chicken tenders with sun-dried tomatoes

	MONDAY	TUESDAY	WEDNESDAY	THURSDAY	FRIDAY	SATURDAY	SUNDAY
BREAKFAST							
LUNCH							
SNACK							
DINNER							
QUICK DINNER							

	MONDAY	TUESDAY	WEDNESDAY	THURSDAY	FRIDAY	SATURDAY	SUNDAY
BREAKFAST	Cantaloupe Wedge with Fruit Topping 6	Plain yogurt swirled with honey and blueberries	whole-grain cold cereal topped with raspberries	grilled Peanut butter and jam on wheat bread	fruit smoothie Havarti cheese melted on a whole-grain roll	Breakfast Fajitas 5	oatmeal topped with sliced strawberries
LUNCH	turkey club sandwich celery sticks	egg salad on Peasant bread with cucumber honeydew wedge	garden salad topped with edamame (frozen soybeans) veggie juice	Caesar salad topped with crabmeat	vegetable soup salad	baked Potato topped with cheddar cheese and broccoli	Cottage Cheese Pancakes 7 with fruit jam
SNACK	watermelon wedge	Pumpernickel rounds topped with Spinach Dip 1	graham crackers Peach	blue sesame corn chips and veggie sticks dipped in melted cheese dip	roasted eggplant spread with Pita wedges	cherries	frozen juice Pop
DINNER	spinach quiche salad	grilled tuna baked Potato steamed broccoli with red pepper strips	chicken Parmesan rice sauteed spinach garlic bread	Pierogies Primavera 15 nectarine	roasted leg of lamb Corn Pudding 29 cucumber and red Pepper salad	sauteed scallops in lemon butter angel hair Pasta steamed green beans	Crispy Dijon Chicken 17 red bliss Potatoes Peas
QUICK DINNER	bean and Pasta soup crostini crackers Peach	Tuna melt 27 baby carrots	Chicken Fajitas 16 with peppers and onions	Potato gnocchi with melted butter and Parmesan cheese grapefruit sections	grilled lamb Patties drizzled with ranch dressing served in whole wheat pitas apple sauce	sauteed scallops served over spring mix	chicken salad with grapes and walnuts on a crusty roll

QUICK DINNER

DINNER

SNACK

LUNCH

BREAKFAST

MONDAY TUESDAY WEDNESDAY THURSDAY FRIDAY SATURDAY SUNDAY

SUMMER

	MONDAY	TUESDAY	WEDNESDAY	THURSDAY	FRIDAY	SATURDAY	SUNDAY
BREAKFAST	Poached eggs on toasted country bread honeydew wedge with lime	oatmeal sprinkled with raisins, brown sugar and cinnamon	apple wedges dipped in yogurt and granola	warm Pumpkin Bread [10] spread with peanut butter half grapefruit	Banana-Berry Smoothie [5] blueberry muffin	whole-grain waffle topped with plain yogurt and raspberries	smoked salmon on a toasted bagel with cream cheese and tomato
LUNCH	Cream Cheese and Salsa Wrap [8]	sliced turkey and fresh mozzarella cheese on Italian bread with roasted peppers and arugula	chopped chef's salad	cold pasta salad with steamed broccoli, olives and grated Parmesan	veggie bacon, lettuce and tomato on rye bread	clam chowder spinach salad	sliced bananas drizzled with honey on whole wheat toast
SNACK	fresh apricots	cold veggies with hummus	bagel chips and string cheese cherries	Pear Popcorn drizzled with olive oil and sprinkled with garlic powder	Peach	diced pineapple and sliced kiwi	a handful of mixed nuts veggie juice
DINNER	broiled scrod with marinara sauce Penne Pasta sauteed Swiss chard	Turkey Meatloaf [19] mashed potatoes sugar snap peas	Homemade Fried Rice [13] salad fruit salad	vegetable omelette sauteed diced potatoes and onions fresh berries	seafood lasagna Italian bread plum	Lemon Chicken [17] rice pilaf steamed green beans	beef and vegetable kabobs cucumber and corn salad
QUICK DINNER	Salmon with Red Onions [26] quick brown rice lettuce wedge	chicken cheese steak with sauteed mushrooms and peppers nectarine	Pasta with Artichoke Hearts and Feta Cheese [14]	chilled strawberry soup deviled eggs breadsticks	shrimp cocktail Pastina salad	Turkey Enchiladas [19]	hamburgers and hot dogs, sliced tomatoes with chopped olives, basil and goat cheese drizzled with balsamic vinaigrette

QUICK DINNER

DINNER

SNACK

LUNCH

BREAKFAST

MONDAY   TUESDAY   WEDNESDAY   THURSDAY   FRIDAY   SATURDAY   SUNDAY

	MONDAY	TUESDAY	WEDNESDAY	THURSDAY	FRIDAY	SATURDAY	SUNDAY
BREAKFAST	strawberries dipped in yogurt and wheat germ	cinnamon raisin French toast topped with maple syrup sliced bananas	cream of wheat topped with soy milk, sprinkled with chopped walnuts and dates	cold whole-grain cereal topped with sliced bananas	fruit kabob	buckwheat pancakes half grapefruit	blueberry blintzes topped with powdered sugar
LUNCH	lean ham and provolone cheese on focaccia with grainy mustard	cottage cheese topped with fresh pineapple	smoked turkey and cheese roll-ups pear	melted cheese and tomato on challah toast	tuna salad with shredded carrots on whole wheat bread	egg salad and baby spinach stuffed in a whole wheat pita	tossed salad topped with baby shrimp
SNACK	frozen grapes	cold veggies with Zucchini and Cheese Dip 2	Lemon-Poppy Seed Loaf 9 with fruit jam	frozen blueberries	tortilla chips with guacamole and salsa	watermelon wedge	cherries
DINNER	Grilled Fresh Tuna Salad 24	Oriental Chicken Kabob 18 salad mango slices	Tomato-Spinach Risotto 15 plum	Pasta Frittata 9 sliced peaches topped with raspberries	baked flounder grilled zucchini and red peppers salad	Stuffed Chicken Breast 18 wild rice salad	Standing Rib Roast 22 scalloped potatoes peas
QUICK DINNER	Italian Tuna, White Bean and Escarole Salad 24	chicken cutlet topped with sliced prosciutto, roasted peppers and fontina cheese	Panzanella with White Beans and Goat Cheese 14 fruit salad	fried eggs rye toast nectarine	Make Your Own Pizza: bay scallops and veggies	turkey Reuben sandwich on sourdough bread	roast beef hoagie with lettuce and tomato

QUICK DINNER

DINNER

SNACK

LUNCH

BREAKFAST

MONDAY TUESDAY WEDNESDAY THURSDAY FRIDAY SATURDAY SUNDAY

	MONDAY	TUESDAY	WEDNESDAY	THURSDAY	FRIDAY	SATURDAY	SUNDAY
BREAKFAST	scrambled eggs toasted English muffin orange wedges	cantaloupe and star fruit salad Carrot muffin 6	whole-grain bagel topped with peach butter	whole-grain cold cereal topped with blueberries	egg white omelette with sauteed mushrooms and onions	whole-grain waffle spread with cashew butter and topped with sliced bananas	apple wedges dipped in peanut butter and honey spread
LUNCH	fresh pear slices with a wedge of brie cheese	cubed turkey and cheese kabob whole-grain crackers strawberries	shrimp salad on pumpernickel bread with lettuce	sliced roast beef on sourdough bread with watercress and horseradish sauce	cream cheese and fruit jam wrap	tomato, fresh mozzarella and basil salad tossed with fresh greens in a balsamic vinaigrette	Caesar salad topped with crabmeat
SNACK	Zucchini Bread 11 spread with almond butter	carrot and celery sticks and corn chips with Hot Bean Dip 1	frozen grapes	plum	cold veggies with Asparagus Dip 1	graham crackers Peach	nectarine
DINNER	Teriyaki Grilled Salmon 27 Parsleyed Potatoes steamed broccoli	veal scallopini buttered noodles sugar snap peas	chicken cacciatore rice salad	Make Your Own Pizza: goat cheese and sun-dried tomatoes	bouillabaisse crusty bread salad	barbecued chicken grille potato wedges grilled zucchini	grilled lamb chops corn on the cob sliced tomatoes
QUICK DINNER	canned salmon over spinach salad	beef stir-fry quick brown rice	Turkey Meatball Sub 19 with tomato sauce and melted provolone	Couscous Salad with Beans and Greens 12	tuna hoagie apple	Chicken Cutlets with Smoked Turkey and Fontina 16 salad	Hearty Pasta Saute 21 lettuce wedge

QUICK DINNER

DINNER

SNACK

LUNCH

BREAKFAST

SUNDAY SATURDAY FRIDAY THURSDAY WEDNESDAY TUESDAY MONDAY

	MONDAY	TUESDAY	WEDNESDAY	THURSDAY	FRIDAY	SATURDAY	SUNDAY
BREAKFAST	cubed mango and kiwi slices sprinkled with blackberries and almonds	Pancakes with maple syrup	crushed pineapple, coconut nectar, banana and tofu shake	fried eggs whole-grain toast fruit kabob	vanilla yogurt topped with fresh berries and wheat germ	whole-grain cold cereal topped with sliced peaches	quiche Lorraine grapefruit sections
LUNCH	raw veggies and soy cheese in a whole wheat pita drizzled with ranch dressing	peanut butter and fruit jam on whole wheat bread	turkey club sandwich sliced apple	tossed salad with edamame (frozen soybeans) toasted pita triangles honeydew cubes	lean ham with lettuce and tomato on a country biscuit	tomato bruschetta plum	Shrimp Wrap with Corn Salsa [26]
SNACK	hard-boiled egg fresh apricot	frozen juice pop	grapes	a handful of pecans veggie juice	cantaloupe cubes	cold veggies with hummus	plain yogurt swirled with honey and sliced strawberries
DINNER	Oven-Baked Fried Fish [25] shoestring potatoes peas pineapple chunks	grilled chicken breast topped with sautéed broccoli rabe and melted provolone cheese	farfalle pasta with spinach and grated cheese fresh berries	wild mushroom risotto salad Italian bread	smoked salmon and cream cheese omelette toasted bagel tomato juice	Sweet and Sour Meatballs [22] potato wedges grilled summer squash and onions	Fast and Easy Chicken Chili [17] corn muffins
QUICK DINNER	Spinach Salad with Shrimp [27]	Zippy Turkey Pesto [19]	angel hair pasta with garlic, olive oil and shredded prosciutto plum	bean tacos with shredded lettuce, cheese and chopped tomatoes	smoked salmon on a bagel with cream cheese and sliced tomato	grilled hamburgers and hot dogs baked beans coleslaw	Pasta Chicken Caesar Salad [18] Italian bread nectarine

QUICK DINNER

DINNER

SNACK

LUNCH

BREAKFAST

MONDAY   TUESDAY   WEDNESDAY   THURSDAY   FRIDAY   SATURDAY   SUNDAY

	MONDAY	TUESDAY	WEDNESDAY	THURSDAY	FRIDAY	SATURDAY	SUNDAY
BREAKFAST	cottage cheese topped with mixed berries	Peach smoothie Energy Muffin 8	whole-grain waffle topped with melted cheese half grapefruit	whole-grain cereal topped with sliced bananas and strawberries	raisin toast topped with honey grapefruit juice	hard-boiled egg Cantaloupe Wedge with Fruit Topping 6	fruit kabob with strawberry yogurt
LUNCH	turkey and pepper Jack cheese on a bagel with Dijon mustard	egg salad on a croissant with sprouts	apple slices spread with almond butter and sprinkled with granola	chilled Gazpacho 3 topped with diced cucumber hummus with pita wedges	tossed salad with flaked tuna and chopped tomatoes	turkey bologna and soy cheese on rye bread with yellow mustard Peach	vegetable Puff with Asiago Cheese 11
SNACK	yellow corn chips with tabbouleh	mini egg rolls	fig cookie glass of milk	a handful of raspberries	cold veggies with onion dip	plum	Popcorn Balls 10
DINNER	scallop scampi herbed couscous steamed string beans	fettuccini topped with sautéed Swiss chard and shaved Parmesan cheese	sesame chicken Jasmine rice with mandarin oranges Honey-Ginger Carrots 29	Barbecued Short Ribs 20 corn on the cob Coleslaw 28	Pierogi Nicoise Salad 25 bread sticks cherries	Make Your Own Pizza: traditional	fried chicken potato salad cucumber salad sliced tomatoes
QUICK DINNER	Shrimp and White Bean Salad 26	bowtie pasta with marinara sauce	chicken steak sandwich with sautéed Portabello mushrooms and Havarti cheese	Zesty Barbecue Pitas 23 raw baby carrots	salmon salad on focaccia blueberries	veggie burger topped with fried onions on a whole-grain bun grapes	Canadian bacon, lettuce and tomato sandwich

QUICK DINNER

DINNER

SNACK

LUNCH

BREAKFAST

MONDAY   TUESDAY   WEDNESDAY   THURSDAY   FRIDAY   SATURDAY   SUNDAY

	MONDAY	TUESDAY	WEDNESDAY	THURSDAY	FRIDAY	SATURDAY	SUNDAY
BREAKFAST	vanilla yogurt topped with fresh pineapple	cheese quesadilla fresh blueberries	whole-grain cold cereal with chopped prunes	Blueberry Breakfast Shake 5 whole-grain toast	oatmeal topped with raisins and brown sugar	scrambled eggs hash browns honeydew wedge	Puffed Pancake 10 topped with sliced bananas
LUNCH	smoked salmon and herb cream cheese tea sandwiches strawberries	turkey on French bread with pesto sauce apple	sliced hard-boiled eggs on rye toast with lettuce	chopped chef's salad	sushi orange slices	fresh fruit salad assorted cheeses crusty bread	chicken salad on a buttermilk biscuit peach
SNACK	graham crackers with peanut butter and jam	celery sticks string cheese black and green olives	cold veggies with eggplant dip	fresh apricot	watermelon cubes	frozen grapes	Chilled Zucchini Soup 3
DINNER	vegetarian chili warm corn bread salad	Pierogies Pesto 14 salad	turkey London broil baked potatoes steamed green beans	barbecued chicken corn on the cob salad cubed mango	lasagna garlic toast salad	grilled shrimp brown rice roasted zucchini and mushrooms	grilled pork chops Sweet Potato and Apple Casserole 31 salad
QUICK DINNER	Panzanella with White Beans and Goat Cheese 14	Linguini with Shrimp Scampi 25 snow pea pods	smoked deli turkey cobb salad	Turkey and Ham Focaccia 23 carrot sticks	Pasta with spinach and chopped tomatoes	Caesar salad topped with crabmeat	beef ravioli with tomato sauce pear

QUICK DINNER

DINNER

SNACK

LUNCH

BREAKFAST

MONDAY TUESDAY WEDNESDAY THURSDAY FRIDAY SATURDAY SUNDAY

	MONDAY	TUESDAY	WEDNESDAY	THURSDAY	FRIDAY	SATURDAY	SUNDAY
BREAKFAST	whole-grain waffles topped with maple syrup and sliced bananas	sliced plums topped with plain yogurt and sprinkled with blackberries	cheese omelette toasted bagel grapes	almond butter and grape jam sandwich	sliced pears with maple yogurt, 9 sprinkled with walnuts	whole-grain cold cereal topped with fresh raspberries	Cheese Blintzes 7 topped with sour cream and blueberries
LUNCH	beef salami cubes dipped in yellow mustard carrot and celery sticks	tuna salad on a croissant with sprouts	hummus and roasted pepper in a whole wheat pita with lettuce	sliced smoked turkey and muenster cheese roll-ups cucumber spears	Pumpkin Bread 10 spread with cream cheese blackberries	lean ham and cheese on focaccia with grainy mustard cantaloupe wedge	tossed salad with chopped veggies whole-grain roll
SNACK	strawberries	Microwaved Baked Apple 9	frozen juice pop	blueberries	popcorn sprinkled with grated Parmesan kiwi slices	cold veggies with thousand island dressing	cherries
DINNER	turkey cutlets Parmesan rice sauteed spinach	Make Your Own Pizza: Primavera 13	spaghetti and meatballs salad garlic bread	Light Crab Cakes 24 roasted potatoes and asparagus half grapefruit	poached eggs on a whole wheat English muffin plum	chicken marsala orzo with diced red pepper salad	Paella salad
QUICK DINNER	Turkey Enchilada 19 sliced peaches	Make Your Own Pizza: black olive and mushroom	Zesty Barbecue Pitas 23	shrimp quesadilla orange and grapefruit sections	white beans with olive oil and spinach	Chicken Fajitas 16 pineapple chunks	seafood chowder oyster crackers fresh apricot

	MONDAY	TUESDAY	WEDNESDAY	THURSDAY	FRIDAY	SATURDAY	SUNDAY
BREAKFAST							
LUNCH							
SNACK							
DINNER							
QUICK DINNER							

	MONDAY	TUESDAY	WEDNESDAY	THURSDAY	FRIDAY	SATURDAY	SUNDAY
BREAKFAST	oatmeal topped with sliced bananas and sprinkled with blueberries	sliced mangos topped with vanilla yogurt whole-grain toast	scoop of cottage cheese topped with mandarin oranges Homemade Trail Mix 8	blueberry muffin half grapefruit	grilled cheese with ham peach	whole wheat pancakes with honey raspberries	lox, onions and scrambled eggs toasted bagel
LUNCH	shrimp cocktail whole-grain crackers	Antipasto Salad 28 crostini crackers	turkey and avocado slices in a whole wheat pita topped with sun-dried tomatoes	egg salad on pumpernickel bread with lettuce and tomato	mini egg rolls	roast beef hoagie with lettuce and tomato	Pita Pizza
SNACK	apple wedges spread with cashew butter sprinkled with wheat germ	cold veggies with Cucumber Dip 1	pear	banana slices topped with peanut butter	orange wedges	cantaloupe and strawberry kabob	frozen grapes
DINNER	Caesar salad topped with grilled chicken breast Italian bread	Beef Fajitas 20 honeydew with lime	swordfish with tomatoes and capers paprika potatoes pineapple chunks	grilled veggie hoagie with fresh mozzarella	barbecued chicken Corn Pudding 29 grilled red onions	Vegetable Lasagna 15 garlic toast salad	seafood stew crusty whole-grain rolls salad
QUICK DINNER	turkey hot dogs baked beans coleslaw	minute steak sandwich on Italian roll with sautéed onions and mushrooms	Tuna Melt 27 raw baby carrots	Cream Cheese and Salsa Wrap 8 sliced plums and apricots	chicken and veggie stir-fry	Linguini with Shrimp Scampi 25 spinach salad	Salmon Baked in Foil 25 salad cherries

	MONDAY	TUESDAY	WEDNESDAY	THURSDAY	FRIDAY	SATURDAY	SUNDAY
BREAKFAST	English muffin with melted cheese sliced kiwi	grapefruit sections topped with yogurt bran muffin	apple wedges spread with peanut butter sprinkled with whole-grain cereal	whole-grain cold cereal with soy milk and raspberries	Hole in One Eggs 8 sliced strawberries	Puffed Pancake 10 sauteed apples	scrambled eggs with herbs Cranberry muffin 7
LUNCH	lean ham on sourdough bread with lettuce, tomato and honey mustard	cream cheese and fruit jam on a whole wheat bagel celery sticks	smoked turkey on a baguette with lettuce, tomato and avocado pineapple chunks	tuna wrap with shredded carrots and cucumber slices sliced papaya	garden salad with chickpeas and red beets	grilled cheese with turkey bacon and sliced red pepper	tomato soup almond butter on crostini crackers
SNACK	Baked Apples 5 with cinnamon and raisins	a handful of pecans veggie juice	cold veggies and Hot Bean Dip 1	Popcorn Balls 10 apple	banana slices dipped in yogurt and wheat germ	bagel chips with herbed cream cheese spread raw baby carrots	fruit chunks and marshmallows dipped in chocolate
DINNER	sauteed turkey cutlets topped with artichoke hearts and sun-dried tomatoes, orzo pasta, steamed green beans	Sweet and Sour Meatballs 22 Spaghetti Squash Saute 30 steamed spinach	Lemon Chicken 17 barley broccoli with black olives	baked striped bass roasted potatoes sauteed shredded zucchini and onions	vegetable Lasagna 15 salad garlic bread	Stuffed Chicken Breast 18 herbed couscous salad	veal roast with onions Honey-Ginger Carrots 29 Steamed Brussels Sprouts 30
QUICK DINNER	sauteed turkey cutlet on focaccia with pesto sauce pear	hamburgers on sesame seed buns coleslaw	chicken quesadilla grapes	Baked Burritos 12 with sour cream and salsa	spinach ravioli with mushroom marinara sauce garlic bread mango slices	shrimp and vegetable stir-fry quick brown rice melon cubes	grilled chicken hoagie with provolone, lettuce and tomato

QUICK DINNER

DINNER

SNACK

LUNCH

BREAKFAST

MONDAY TUESDAY WEDNESDAY THURSDAY FRIDAY SATURDAY SUNDAY

	MONDAY	TUESDAY	WEDNESDAY	THURSDAY	FRIDAY	SATURDAY	SUNDAY
BREAKFAST	scoop of cottage cheese raisin pecan bread with peach butter	multi-grain hot cereal with sliced bananas	yogurt drizzled with honey and walnuts half grapefruit	mushroom egg white omelette toasted croissant	Pumpkin muffin 10 spread with peanut butter	whole-grain toast topped with gouda cheese and sliced pears	jelly crepes sprinkled with powdered sugar
LUNCH	mushroom barley soup Havarti cheese on poppy seed crackers	egg salad on a sesame bagel with sprouts	roast beef on rye bread with coleslaw and thousand island dressing watermelon cubes	mixed greens topped with cucumber slices and crumbled feta cheese pita triangles	smoked turkey wrap with lettuce, tomato and grainy mustard	veggie burger on a whole-grain bun with lettuce and tomato	sushi orange wedges
SNACK	celery sticks with chunky veggie dip	golden delicious apple slices with a wedge of brie cheese	whole edamame (frozen soybeans) tomato juice	oatmeal raisin cookie glass of milk	frozen grapes	carrot sticks with onion dip	celery sticks and endive leaves with roasted red pepper hummus
DINNER	Fast and Easy Chicken Chili 17 warm corn bread salad	swordfish with tomatoes and capers mashed sweet potatoes	turkey scallopini orzo pasta with peas	Tomato-Spinach Risotto 15	Pot roast with potatoes, onions and carrots	Light Crab Cakes 24 acorn squash green beans	Chicken Fajitas 16 served with guacamole and sour cream
QUICK DINNER	Pasta Chicken Caesar Salad 18 crusty bread	Pierogi Nicoise Salad 25 orange wedges	turkey sloppy joe raw baby carrots	Potato gnocchi with sauteed spinach and sun-dried tomatoes	minute steak sandwich on a long roll with tomato sauce and fried onions	crab quesadilla apple	tofu franks barbecued baked beans salad

QUICK DINNER

DINNER

SNACK

LUNCH

BREAKFAST

MONDAY
TUESDAY
WEDNESDAY
THURSDAY
FRIDAY
SATURDAY
SUNDAY

	MONDAY	TUESDAY	WEDNESDAY	THURSDAY	FRIDAY	SATURDAY	SUNDAY
BREAKFAST	apple wedges spread with peanut butter and sprinkled with wheat germ	cottage cheese with diced cantaloupe banana bread	fried eggs on a toasted bagel strawberries	multi-grain cold cereal with soymilk and fresh berries	whole-grain waffles with maple syrup half grapefruit	orange sections, kiwi and banana slices topped with vanilla yogurt and sprinkled with pecans	challah French toast dusted with powdered sugar microwaved Baked Apple 9
LUNCH	turkey slices wrapped around carrot sticks dipped in mustard-mayonnaise, melba toast, grapes	wagon wheel pasta salad with diced ham, tomato, and peas in vinaigrette	tuna salad with diced apples on sourdough bread with lettuce	smoked mozzarella cheese on crusty bread with tomato and honey mustard	hummus on toasted whole wheat English muffin topped with yellow pepper rings	turkey bologna on whole wheat with lettuce and mustard	cashew butter and peach preserves on toasted raisin bread
SNACK	pear	orange a handful of sunflower seeds	raw veggies with zucchini and Cheese Dip 2	tortilla chips with guacamole	fontina cheese cubes with spicy brown mustard	apple sauce with cinnamon	popcorn sprinkled with Parmesan cheese
DINNER	grilled lamb chops brown rice stir-fried broccoli rabe	sesame chicken hot apples and cranberry sauce steamed green beans	spinach tortellini with diced tomatoes garlic bread	Salmon Baked in Foil 25 rice Coleslaw 28	Pork tenderloin Sweet Potato and Apple Casserole 31 salad	chicken cacciatore roasted zucchini, summer squash and onions Italian bread	bouillabaisse roasted potatoes garlic cheese toast
QUICK DINNER	beef taco salad	minestrone soup sautéed chicken cutlet salad	baked polenta with marinara sauce and mozzarella cheese	manhattan clam chowder oyster crackers grapes	hot deli roast beef sandwich carrot and celery sticks	Turkey Enchilada 19 pineapple chunks	Linguini with Shrimp Scampi 25 salad

QUICK DINNER

DINNER

SNACK

LUNCH

BREAKFAST

MONDAY   TUESDAY   WEDNESDAY   THURSDAY   FRIDAY   SATURDAY   SUNDAY

	MONDAY	TUESDAY	WEDNESDAY	THURSDAY	FRIDAY	SATURDAY	SUNDAY
BREAKFAST	crushed pineapple, coconut nectar and banana tofu shake graham crackers	toasted bagel spread with garden vegetable cream cheese cantaloupe wedge	apple wedges with cubed cheddar cheese multi-grain toast	Zucchini Bread [11] served warm with sweet cream butter orange slices	baked pears sprinkled with granola	Cottage Cheese Pancakes [7] sautéed apple slices	whole-grain cold cereal with soy milk kiwi and mango slices
LUNCH	roast beef on French bread with horseradish sauce Pear	smoked turkey on pumpernickel bread with cranberry relish	vegetable soup crusty bread	tuna salad stuffed pita with lettuce and tomato	turkey roll-ups whole-grain crackers strawberries	celery stuffed with peanut butter rolled in raisins and coconut	open face melted Monterey Jack cheese with tomato and guacamole
SNACK	broccoli and cauliflower florets with warm cheese dip	banana slices dipped in wheat germ	frozen grapes	cold veggies with veggie Dip [2]	whole edamame (frozen soybeans) veggie juice	bagel chips and carrots with hummus	popcorn raspberries
DINNER	grilled skewered chicken with satay dip fine egg noodles salad	beef and rice stuffed green peppers	baked flounder roasted potatoes with fresh thyme glazed carrots	four-cheese ravioli with mushroom tomato sauce salad	chicken pot pie salad	Homemade Fried Rice [13] sautéed cherry tomatoes salad	veal stew salad crusty bread
QUICK DINNER	turkey franks vegetarian baked beans coleslaw	French toast veggie Canadian bacon fresh figs	Shrimp and White Bean Salad [26]	linguini with broccoli, walnuts and Parmesan cheese Italian bread	Make Your Own Pizza: diced tomatoes and artichoke hearts	scrambled eggs hash browns rye toast half grapefruit	chopped salad crusty bread

	QUICK DINNER	DINNER	SNACK	LUNCH	BREAKFAST
MONDAY					
TUESDAY					
WEDNESDAY					
THURSDAY					
FRIDAY					
SATURDAY					
SUNDAY					

	MONDAY	TUESDAY	WEDNESDAY	THURSDAY	FRIDAY	SATURDAY	SUNDAY
BREAKFAST	whole wheat scones with jam / vanilla yogurt sprinkled with pecans	egg white omelette with avocado and salsa / fresh figs	oatmeal sprinkled with nutmeg and chopped dates	cinnamon French toast topped with sautéed pears	raisin toast with melted soy cheese / papaya slices	apple blintzes topped with sour cream and jam	Cranberry Bread with warmed apple sauce
LUNCH	tuna wrap with cucumber slices and shredded carrots	Peanut butter and jam tea sandwiches / Pear	turkey bologna on rye bread with yellow mustard / grapes	raw veggies and pita wedges dipped in hummus	egg salad with cashews on country white bread	Pizza bagel	fruit salad with a scoop of cottage cheese / melba toast
SNACK	veggie pepperoni and soy cheese slices	warm apple cider	tortilla chips with baba ghanoush dip	tomato soup / oyster crackers	pineapple, strawberries and banana chunks dipped in chocolate fondu	Plain yogurt swirled with a teaspoon of fruit preserves	a handful of peanuts / tomato juice
DINNER	vegetable Lasagna 15 / Antipasto Salad 28	sautéed sea scallops / wild mushroom risotto / Caesar salad	sautéed turkey cutlet with tomato sauce and shredded mozzarella / orzo pasta / steamed broccoli	veggie burger / apple and mozzarella salad	Paella / bibb lettuce with mandarin oranges	filet of beef / creamed corn / Roasted Asparagus with Cheese and Pine Nuts 29	Pot roasted chicken with potatoes and carrots
QUICK DINNER	Pasta with Tomatoes and Olives 14 / garlic toast	Oven-Baked Fried Fish 25 / coleslaw / Potato salad	Chicken and Artichokes 16 / orzo pasta	bean and cheese enchilada	Tuna Melt 27 / garden salad	Turkey and Ham Focaccia 23 / carrots and celery sticks	open face smoked turkey and melted fontina cheese sandwich / pineapple cubes

	QUICK DINNER	DINNER	SNACK	LUNCH	BREAKFAST
MONDAY					
TUESDAY					
WEDNESDAY					
THURSDAY					
FRIDAY					
SATURDAY					
SUNDAY					

	MONDAY	TUESDAY	WEDNESDAY	THURSDAY	FRIDAY	SATURDAY	SUNDAY
BREAKFAST	whole-grain cold cereal with soy milk sprinkled with fresh berries and slivered almonds	Breakfast Fajitas [5] orange slices	toasted raisin pecan bread with peach butter wedge of gouda cheese	whole-grain hot cereal with sliced bananas	cottage cheese with orange and grapefruit sections Lemon-Poppy Seed Muffin [9]	apple wedges spread with almond butter sprinkled with granola	Poached eggs on an English muffin with soy Canadian bacon pineapple and mango slices
LUNCH	lean ham and melon cubes whole-grain crackers	chopped salad of lettuce, tomato and cucumber topped with feta cheese	shrimp salad on rye bread with lettuce	tuna salad stuffed cherry tomatoes baby carrots and olives	turkey and cheese cubes dipped in champagne mustard	grilled cheese with tomato lettuce wedge	sushi orange wedges
SNACK	carrot sticks with Asparagus Dip [1]	celery stuffed with peanut butter	split pea soup with croutons and Parmesan cheese	cauliflower florets and endive with thousand island dip	Butternut Squash Soup [3] French bread	frozen banana slices	toasted pumpkin seeds veggie juice
DINNER	tuna noodle casserole salad	Turkey Meatloaf, [19] baked sweet potatoes with cinnamon and brown sugar, steamed green beans	vegetarian chili corn muffins	grilled pork chops Sweet Potato and Apple Casserole [31] salad	Couscous Salad with Beans and Greens [12]	baked chicken barley with sauteed spinach and roasted red peppers salad	grilled New York strip steak fingerling potatoes sugar snap peas
QUICK DINNER	seafood chowder salad crusty bread	Zippy Turkey Pesto [19]	Make Your Own Pizza: Mexican [13]	turkey bacon, lettuce and tomato on whole wheat toast	Pierogies Pesto [14] half grapefruit	chicken and veggie stir-fry quick brown rice	beef burritos with sour cream and salsa

QUICK DINNER

DINNER

SNACK

LUNCH

BREAKFAST

MONDAY

TUESDAY

WEDNESDAY

THURSDAY

FRIDAY

SATURDAY

SUNDAY

AUTUMN

	MONDAY	TUESDAY	WEDNESDAY	THURSDAY	FRIDAY	SATURDAY	SUNDAY
BREAKFAST	warm oatmeal sprinkled with cinnamon and nutmeg half grapefruit	sliced Pears with Maple Yogurt 9	toasted Peanut butter and jam sandwich	warm brioche with sweet cream butter and jam cantaloupe wedge	buttermilk waffles topped with sautéed apples	Hole in One Eggs 8 strawberries	whole-grain cold cereal with sliced banana
LUNCH	cashew butter and apple slices on whole-grain bread	chicken salad with grapes on whole wheat crackers	ham and cream cheese roll-ups apple	smoked turkey on pumpernickel bread with lettuce, tomato, cucumber and mustard	fruit salad topped with cottage cheese and plain yogurt	chicken noodle soup whole-grain roll	salmon salad on focaccia
SNACK	popcorn	cold veggies with honey mustard dip	banana bread	Homemade Trail Mix 8 tomato juice	carrot-raisin salad	string cheese grapes	hot chocolate with marshmallows
DINNER	roasted turkey breast with cranberry sauce stuffing carrot puree	beef and vegetable kabob baked potato	Pasta Frittata 9 salad	grilled ginger tuna brown rice snow pea pods	chicken piccata sweet potato sautéed escarole	Barbecued Short Ribs 20 Corn Pudding 29 steamed green beans	whole wheat Penne with Quick and Easy Ratatouille 29 chopped apple salad
QUICK DINNER	Turkey Meatball Sub 19 salad	minute steak on a long roll with tomato sauce and fried onions	Pasta with Artichoke Hearts and Feta Cheese 14 garlic bread	Shrimp Wrap with Corn Salsa 26	hot deli turkey sandwich with gravy instant mashed potatoes steamed spinach	roast beef hoagie	Cream Cheese and Salsa Wrap 8

	MONDAY	TUESDAY	WEDNESDAY	THURSDAY	FRIDAY	SATURDAY	SUNDAY
BREAKFAST							
LUNCH							
SNACK							
DINNER							
QUICK DINNER							

	MONDAY	TUESDAY	WEDNESDAY	THURSDAY	FRIDAY	SATURDAY	SUNDAY
BREAKFAST	warm buckwheat cereal drizzled with honey honeydew wedge	whole-grain cereal with soy milk and chopped prunes	cinnamon raisin French toast	farmer's cheese spread on whole-grain bread topped with sliced pear	raisin pecan bread spread with apple butter	fruit and yogurt smoothie	Western omelette hash brown potatoes
LUNCH	tuna with diced apples on raisin bread	corned beef with coleslaw and Russian dressing on rye bread	pineapple cubes and orange and grapefruit sections topped with cottage cheese, sprinkled with walnuts	seafood salad on a croissant with lettuce	hard-boiled egg tossed salad	mixed greens with crumbled goat cheese and grape tomatoes	mushroom barley soup whole-grain crackers
SNACK	cold veggies and White Bean Dip [2]	cantaloupe cubes topped with raspberries	Zucchini Bread [11] with fruit jam	fresh figs	whole edamame (frozen soybeans) veggie juice	mini egg rolls	Pumpkin Muffins [10] spread with pear butter
DINNER	spaghetti with Tiny Meatballs [23] salad Italian bread	Teriyaki Grilled Salmon [27] Potatoes au gratin mixed veggies	curry chicken rice steamed green beans	Roasted Potatoes Topped with Sun-Dried Tomato Pesto [30] salad fruit salad	Squash and Chard Chili [22] warm corn bread	seafood stew crusty bread salad	chicken Kiev basmati rice peas
QUICK DINNER	sloppy joe cucumber spears	Make Your Own Pizza: smoked salmon and brie cheese salad	Chicken Cutlets with Smoked Turkey and Fontina [16] raw baby carrots	gnocchi with spinach and sun-dried tomatoes	Hearty Pasta Saute [21] garlic bread	Tuna Melt [27] coleslaw pickles and olives	tofu franks vegetarian baked beans grapes

QUICK DINNER

DINNER

SNACK

LUNCH

BREAKFAST

MONDAY

TUESDAY

WEDNESDAY

THURSDAY

FRIDAY

SATURDAY

SUNDAY

	MONDAY	TUESDAY	WEDNESDAY	THURSDAY	FRIDAY	SATURDAY	SUNDAY
BREAKFAST	Baked Apples 5 with warm maple syrup	cream of wheat with raisins and honey	melted cheddar cheese on whole-grain toast half grapefruit	scrambled eggs toasted sesame bagel orange slices	grilled cheese and tomato grapes	granola cereal warm apple cider	Energy Muffins 8
LUNCH	turkey bologna wrap with lettuce, tomato and mayo-mustard	walnut butter and banana slices on whole wheat bread	vegetable soup whole-grain crackers and cheese	turkey and apple slices in pita with honey mustard	roast beef roll-ups rye crackers coleslaw	sushi garden salad with ginger dressing	egg salad on pumpernickel bread with sliced tomato
SNACK	tortilla chips with salsa	cold veggies with Cucumber Dip 1	nachos with black beans	split pea soup oyster crackers Pear	a handful of pecans and pistachios veggie juice	hot chocolate with marshmallows	cheese and crackers
DINNER	Grilled Fresh Tuna Salad 24 Pineapple chunks	veal Piccata Pastina Broccoli in Creamy Balsamic Sauce 28	Teriyaki London Broil 23 quinoa salad	Pierogies Primavera 15	Make Your Own Pizza: shrimp and veggie	Antipasto Salad 28 crusty country bread	Standing Rib Roast 22 pureed turnips steamed green beans popovers
QUICK DINNER	Scallops with Almonds 26 quick brown rice salad	veal patty on a whole-grain bun with lettuce and tomato	Turkey Meatball Sub 19 lettuce wedge	cheese ravioli with pesto sauce cold cauliflower florets	linguini with clam sauce salad	tofu and veggie stir-fry	tacos with shredded lettuce, tomato and olives

	MONDAY	TUESDAY	WEDNESDAY	THURSDAY	FRIDAY	SATURDAY	SUNDAY
BREAKFAST							
LUNCH							
SNACK							
DINNER							
QUICK DINNER							

	MONDAY	TUESDAY	WEDNESDAY	THURSDAY	FRIDAY	SATURDAY	SUNDAY
BREAKFAST	warm millet cereal with slivered almonds and soy milk orange sections	crushed pineapple, coconut nectar and banana shake	multi-grain cold cereal with raspberries	poached eggs on an English muffin with Canadian bacon cantaloupe cubes	cottage cheese topped with sliced strawberries graham crackers	challah French toast dusted with powdered sugar half grapefruit	Cheddar Cornmeal Waffles with Salsa 6 topped with diced avocado
LUNCH	shrimp salad in a tomato half sesame crackers grapes	beef salami and Muenster cheese cubes dipped in spicy mustard Pear	turkey breast on rye bread with lettuce and tomato	whole wheat pita stuffed with hummus, tomato slices and sprouts	lentil soup carrot muffin 6	cold pasta primavera salad	chopped chef's salad
SNACK	cold veggies with veggie Dip 2	veggie sticks and bagel chips with Hot Bean Dip 1	apple sauce sprinkled with cinnamon	popcorn	plain yogurt sprinkled with granola and dried cranberries	frozen banana slices	pear wedges drizzled with honey
DINNER	Crispy Dijon Chicken 17 shoestring potatoes sauteed carrots	stuffed shells with tomato sauce salad garlic bread	chili warm corn bread salad	Oriental Chicken Kabobs 18 served over rice steamed broccoli	Salmon with Red Onions 26 scalloped potatoes sauteed zucchini	beef stew basmati rice salad peasant bread	vegetable puff with Asiago Cheese 11
QUICK DINNER	chicken quesadilla avocado and tomato salad	vermicelli with spinach and pine nuts in garlic olive oil Italian bread	beef burritos with sour cream and salsa	chicken steak sandwich on a long roll with melted mozzarella	salmon cakes on a whole-grain bun with cocktail sauce celery and carrot sticks	meatball sandwich with marinara sauce and melted provolone cheese	smoked salmon on a toasted bagel with cream cheese and tomato

	BREAKFAST	LUNCH	SNACK	DINNER	QUICK DINNER
MONDAY					
TUESDAY					
WEDNESDAY					
THURSDAY					
FRIDAY					
SATURDAY					
SUNDAY					

	BREAKFAST	LUNCH	SNACK	DINNER	QUICK DINNER
MONDAY	Hole in One Eggs 8 / mandarin oranges	cream cheese and strawberry jam wrap	kiwi and mango slices	steamed red snapper / Parsleyed new potatoes / snow pea pods	Fresh Tuna Burger 24 on a whole-grain bun / apple sauce / raw baby carrots
TUESDAY	whole-grain waffles spread with almond butter and topped with sliced bananas	Warm Carrot Soup 4 / salad	a handful of walnuts / tomato juice	barbecued chicken / rice / steamed green beans	Capered Chicken Cutlets 16 on focaccia
WEDNESDAY	multi-grain cold cereal with chopped dates	Smoked turkey and Havarti cheese wrap with lettuce and champagne mustard	apple wedges dipped in honey	Hearty Pasta Sauté 21	Zesty Barbecue Pitas 23
THURSDAY	string cheese	tuna salad with shredded carrots on sourdough bread	pear	turkey burger on a kaiser roll with lettuce and tomato	deli turkey roll with pesto mayonnaise and American cheese whole-grain roll
FRIDAY	toasted bagel with fruit jam / oat bran muffin	lean ham and cheddar cheese on a biscuit with sliced apple	watermelon / graham crackers	Pasta with red clam sauce / garlic toast / grapes	Spinach Salad with Shrimp 27 / whole-grain roll
SATURDAY	scrambled eggs / Banana-Berry Smoothie 5 / whole-grain toast	roast beef hoagie	cold veggies with hummus / black and green olives	mac and Cheese 13 / stewed tomatoes	Baked Burritos 12 / grapefruit sections
SUNDAY	buckwheat pancakes with sautéed pears / strawberries	pizza bagel / orange sections	banana slices dipped in wheat germ	Baked Breaded Chicken 16 / twice-baked potatoes / sautéed zucchini	sautéed chicken tenders with peppers and onions on a long roll

	MONDAY	TUESDAY	WEDNESDAY	THURSDAY	FRIDAY	SATURDAY	SUNDAY
BREAKFAST							
LUNCH							
SNACK							
DINNER							
QUICK DINNER							

	MONDAY	TUESDAY	WEDNESDAY	THURSDAY	FRIDAY	SATURDAY	SUNDAY
BREAKFAST	toasted peanut butter and jam sandwich	five-grain hot cereal with nutmeg and raisins	hard-boiled egg cinnamon toast half grapefruit	whole-grain cold cereal with sliced bananas	Plain yogurt with a swirl of maple syrup and topped with walnuts blueberry muffin	Baked Apples 5 with pecans and raisins	buttermilk waffles with jam papaya cubes
LUNCH	mushroom barley soup sesame crackers	corned beef on rye bread with mustard apple	fruit salad gouda cheese cubes dipped in spicy mustard whole-grain roll	garden salad topped with a scoop of egg salad	turkey breast and Muenster cheese on an onion roll with mustard-mayo sauce pear slices	grilled cheese and tomato on whole-grain bread	salad with flaked tuna and chopped tomatoes
SNACK	mango slices	pineapple and strawberry kabob	whole-wheat pita triangles and celery sticks dipped in baba ghanoush	oatmeal cookie glass of milk	Cranberry Bread 7	hot chocolate with marshmallows	kiwi slices dipped in vanilla yogurt
DINNER	Linguini with Shrimp Scampi 25 salad Italian bread	vegetarian chili warm corn bread salad	pot roasted chicken with potatoes and carrots	baked ziti salad garlic toast	beef brisket roasted potatoes Carrot Souffle 28	baked striped bass quinoa sauteed zucchini and cherry tomatoes	Lemon Chicken 17 noodle pudding Roasted Asparagus with Cheese and Pine Nuts 29
QUICK DINNER	Pierogi Nicoise Salad 25 Italian bread	Cream Cheese and Salsa Wrap 8	grilled chicken wrap with spinach and brie cheese cucumber salad	spaghetti with garlic and olive oil sauteed escarole	hot deli roast beef sandwich with gravy salad	clam chowder tomato and mozzarella salad	Zippy Turkey Pesto 19 avocado and tomato salsa

	MONDAY	TUESDAY	WEDNESDAY	THURSDAY	FRIDAY	SATURDAY	SUNDAY
BREAKFAST							
LUNCH							
SNACK							
DINNER							
QUICK DINNER							

	MONDAY	TUESDAY	WEDNESDAY	THURSDAY	FRIDAY	SATURDAY	SUNDAY
BREAKFAST	whole-grain cold cereal topped with sliced strawberries and soy milk	Pineapple cubes and orange sections topped with yogurt and sprinkled with granola	whole-grain waffles with melted cheddar cheese Pear slices	apple wedges spread with cashew butter sprinkled with wheat germ	oatmeal sprinkled with cinnamon and brown sugar honeydew wedge	Cheese Blintzes 7 topped with raisins and nuts	smoked salmon and herbed cream cheese on a toasted bagel with tomato
LUNCH	chopped veggie salad Pita triangles dipped in hummus	turkey on rye bread with thousand island dressing	cottage cheese topped with fresh fruit, sprinkled with sunflower seeds celery and carrot sticks	warm pea soup topped with croutons	lean ham and cheese roll-ups dipped in grainy mustard Pear	Peanut butter and fruit jam on challah toast	chicken salad with grapes on a croissant
SNACK	banana slices dipped in melted chocolate	graham crackers with peanut butter and jam	frozen grapes	cold veggies with onion dip	veggie sticks and tortilla chips with melted cheese dip	a handful of whole-grain cereal banana	whole edamame (frozen soybeans) veggie juice
DINNER	broiled sirloin steak Roasted Root Vegetables 30 salad	broiled salmon wild rice steamed broccoli with black olives	Stuffed Chicken Breast 18 egg noodles steamed spinach	veal scallopini Potato gnocchi with butter and Parmesan cheese salad	Pasta with tomatoes, Kalamata olives and feta cheese garlic bread	scallop stir-fry brown rice	vegetable Lasagna 15 Italian bread
QUICK DINNER	taco salad tomato and corn salsa	Light Crab Cakes 24 coleslaw Potato salad	Chicken Fajitas 16 served with guacamole and sour cream	chopped chef's salad	Make Your Own Pizza: Kalamata olives and feta cheese	flaked canned tuna tossed with roasted red peppers, basil and olive oil kiwi slices	French toast turkey sausage orange slices

QUICK DINNER

DINNER

SNACK

LUNCH

BREAKFAST

MONDAY TUESDAY WEDNESDAY THURSDAY FRIDAY SATURDAY SUNDAY

Dips

Asparagus Dip

(makes 2 1/4 cups)

1 lb. asparagus (tough ends removed), cut into 1" pieces,
or 1 (10 oz.) package frozen asparagus cuts
1/4 red onion
1 clove of garlic
1 tbs. lemon juice
1 tsp. salt-free vegetable seasoning
2-3 tbs. non-fat yogurt
1 tbs. grated Parmesan cheese
1 tomato, peeled, seeded and chopped

Steam asparagus for about 4-5 minutes. Drain well and cool. After
asparagus has cooled, place it along with onion, garlic, lemon juice and
vegetable seasoning in a food processor or blender. Process until finely
chopped. Add yogurt and grated cheese. Blend and chill.
To serve, place in a bowl and
top with chopped tomatoes.

Cucumber Dip

(makes 1 1/2 cups)

1 cup cottage cheese
(low-fat is fine)
1 cucumber, peeled,
seeded and sliced
1 small white onion, sliced
2 tsp. lemon juice
1 tsp. dried dill
(or 1 tbs. fresh dill, chopped)
1/2 tsp. vegetable seasoning

Mix all ingredients together in a food processor or blender. Process until
smooth. Chill until ready to serve.

Hot Bean Dip

(makes 1 1/2 cups)

1 (14 oz.) can vegetarian refried beans
1 tbs. finely chopped green bell pepper
1 tsp. dehydrated onion flakes
1/4 tsp. garlic powder
a few drops of hot pepper sauce (optional)
1-2 tsp. taco sauce
1/2 cup non-fat yogurt

In a one-quart casserole, stir together all of the ingredients except the
yogurt. Cover and microwave on high for 5 minutes, stirring one time
during cooking. Remove from the microwave and blend in yogurt. Serve
hot with crudité or tortilla chips.

Spinach Dip

(makes 2 1/2 cups)

2 (10 oz.) packages frozen chopped spinach, defrosted and drained
4 canned water chestnuts, quartered
1/2 small onion, sliced
1 cup nonfat yogurt
2 tbs. light mayonnaise
2 tbs. dehydrated vegetable flakes
1/4 tsp. dried thyme, crushed
grated nutmeg

Place all ingredients into a food processor or blender. Process until finely
chopped. Chill until ready to serve.

Vegetable-Yogurt Dip

1 cup plain low-fat yogurt
1 tsp. fresh or dried parsley or dill
1/4 cup chopped vegetables (peppers, carrots, celery)

Mix together and serve.

Veggie Dip

4 oz. tofu cream cheese at room temperature
4 oz. tofu sour cream
half of a (10 oz.) package chopped frozen spinach,
thawed and squeezed dry
1 (4 oz.) can sliced water chestnuts, drained and chopped fine
2 scallions, thinly sliced
1/2 small red bell pepper, cored, seeded and chopped fine
1 tsp. lemon juice
1 tsp. drained horseradish
1 tsp. coarse salt

Beat cream cheese and sour cream together in a medium bowl until smooth. Stir in remaining ingredients and blend well. Cover and refrigerate at least 1 hour and up to 2 days.

White Bean Dip

1 (16 oz.) can white beans, drained but moist
1 clove of garlic, peeled
salt and pepper
2 tbs. plus 1 tsp. extra virgin olive oil
1 tsp. minced fresh rosemary or thyme, or 2 tsp. ground cumin
sprig of fresh rosemary or thyme for garnish

Place beans, garlic and some salt in the container of the food processor. Turn on and add 2 tablespoons olive oil in a steady stream through the feed tube. Process until smooth. Taste and adjust with salt and pepper. Cover and refrigerate (up to 2 days) until 1 hour before serving. Just before serving, stir in herbs, drizzle remaining olive oil and garnish with herb sprig. Serve with chips and cut-up raw vegetables.

Zucchini and Cheese Dip

1 1/4 cup shredded zucchini
3/4 cup shredded cheddar cheese
2 tbs. shredded mozzarella cheese
1/2 cup mayonnaise
2 tbs. sour cream
1/4 cup chopped pecans
2 tbs. finely diced red bell pepper
salt and pepper, to taste

Combine all ingredients and chill for at least 1 hour before serving.

Soups

Butternut Squash Soup

(serves 6-8)

2 1/2 lbs. butternut squash, halved and seeded
1 tbs. olive oil
1 medium onion, diced
2 cloves garlic, minced
ground nutmeg
1 tsp. cinnamon
5-6 cups chicken or vegetable stock
3 Yukon gold potatoes, peeled and chopped
salt and pepper to taste
fresh chives, chopped (optional)

Preheat oven to 400°. Cut squash lengthwise and scoop out the seeds. On a greased baking sheet, place the squash cavity side down and roast for 1 hour. Squash should be soft. Allow to cool. Scoop out flesh into a medium bowl. Heat olive oil in a large stock pot and sauté onions until translucent. Add the garlic, cinnamon and nutmeg and continue to sauté for another minute. Add the roasted squash, chopped potatoes and stock and bring to a boil. Reduce heat and simmer covered with a lid until vegetables are soft. Purée soup with a hand blender in the pot, or transfer to a blender or food processor. Season with salt and pepper to taste. Sprinkle chopped chives on top if desired.

Chilled Zucchini Soup

(serves 2)

3 cups diced zucchini
1 cup fresh basil leaves
1 (14.5 oz.) can chicken broth
1/3 cup reduced-fat buttermilk

In a blender or food processor, chop basil and zucchini until finely minced. Add chicken broth and buttermilk and purée until smooth. Serve chilled.

Cold Pea Soup

(serves 4)

1 lb. peas in the shell, snow peas or sugar snap peas (fresh or frozen)
3 cups chicken or vegetable stock
salt and pepper to taste
1/4 cup heavy or sour cream
chopped parsley (optional)

In a medium saucepan, combine peas and stock. Bring to a boil over medium-high heat. Reduce heat and simmer for about 10 minutes until peas are bright green and tender. Cool slightly for a few minutes. If you are using regular peas, remove a few from their shells for garnish. Refrigerate these until serving. Pour the cooked peas and stock from the saucepan into a blender or food processor and purée. Add salt and pepper to taste. Over a large bowl, use a fine strainer to strain out any solids. Stir cream or sour cream into the bowl of pea purée. Refrigerate before serving. Garnish with reserved peas or chopped parsley. (Can be refrigerated for up to 2 days.)

Gazpacho

1 small onion, cut into 4 pieces
1 large green bell pepper, cored, seeded and cut into 4 pieces
1/2 cup V-8 juice
3 medium tomatoes, cored and cut into 4 pieces each
1 small cucumber, peeled and cut into 4 pieces
2 cloves garlic, peeled
1/2 cup olive oil
1/4 cup white vinegar
salt and pepper to taste
1/4 tsp. Tabasco sauce (optional)
1/2 tsp. Worcestershire sauce

In a blender or food processor, combine onion, pepper and V-8 juice and blend just until chunky. Pour mixture into a large bowl. Blend remaining ingredients quickly and add to the large bowl. Stir two mixtures together and chill for several hours.

Tomato and Bean Soup

(serves 2)

2 tsp. olive oil
1 cup chopped onion
3 cloves garlic, minced
2 (14.5 oz.) cans whole tomatoes, undrained and chopped
2 (16 oz.) cans beans (cannellini or navy beans)
1 (14.5 oz.) can chicken broth
1 tbs. chopped fresh parsley
3/4 tsp. dried oregano
1/4 tsp. pepper
1/4 cup grated Parmesan cheese

Heat olive oil in a large soup pot over medium heat. Add onions and sauté until translucent, about 3 minutes. Add garlic and sauté 1 more minute. Add tomatoes, beans, chicken broth, parsley, oregano and pepper. Bring to a boil and then reduce heat and simmer for 10 minutes. Serve in bowls sprinkled with grated cheese.

Warm Carrot Soup

(serves 12)

1 tsp. olive oil
1 red onion, chopped
2 cloves garlic, minced
2 lbs. carrots (about 12 medium), peeled and chopped
3 medium potatoes, peeled and chopped
5 cups chicken or vegetable stock
1 bay leaf
salt and pepper to taste
fresh dill

Heat olive oil in large stock pot. Sauté onions until translucent, about 3 minutes. Add garlic. Add the remaining ingredients and 4 cups of the stock. Simmer partially covered for about 30-40 minutes until vegetables are tender. Remove the bay leaf. Purée soup with a hand blender in the pot, or transfer to a blender or food processor. Add the remaining 1 cup of stock and stir. Add salt and pepper to taste.

Eggs, Breads, Muffins and Snacks

Baked Apples

4 apples
1/4 cup brown sugar
2 tbs. raisins
ground cinnamon

Preheat oven to 400°. Wash and core apples. Place in a baking dish. Fill apple centers with about 1 tbs. brown sugar, 5 raisins and a sprinkle of cinnamon. Pour 1/2 inch of water into the baking dish and cover. Bake for 25 minutes. Serve warm.

Banana Nut Bread

(makes 1 loaf)

2 cups unbleached all-purpose flour
1 cup whole wheat pastry flour
2 tsp. baking powder
1 tsp. baking soda
1 tsp. ground cinnamon
1/2 tsp. salt
1/4 tsp. ground nutmeg
3 very ripe bananas, peeled
1/3 cup butter or margarine, softened
3/4 cup maple syrup
1 tbs. fresh lemon juice
1 tbs. vanilla extract
1 cup walnuts, toasted and chopped

Preheat oven to 350°. Lightly oil a 9" x 5" loaf pan. In a medium bowl, combine flours, baking powder, baking soda, cinnamon, salt and nutmeg. Set aside. In a large bowl, mash bananas until creamy. Add butter or margarine and combine with bananas. Stir in the maple syrup, lemon juice, vanilla and nuts. Using a rubber spatula, fold the dry ingredients into the wet mixture. Combine but do not over mix. Pour batter into the prepared loaf pan and gently smooth the top with the spatula. Bake in the oven for 1 hour or until toothpick inserted into middle of the loaf comes out clean. Cool in the pan for thirty minutes and then turn loaf onto a wire rack to cool completely.

Banana-Berry Smoothie

1 banana
1/2 cup blueberries (fresh or frozen)
1/2 carton berry-flavored yogurt
2-3 tbs. orange juice
ice

Add all ingredients to the blender and blend. Pour in a glass and serve.

Blueberry Breakfast Shake

(serves 2)

1/2 cup blueberries, rinsed
1/2 cup low-fat vanilla yogurt
1/2 cup skim milk
2 tbs. honey
5 ice cubes

Place all ingredients in a blender and process until smooth. Serve immediately.

Breakfast Fajitas

flour tortillas
scrambled eggs
salsa
grated Monterey jack cheese
sliced black olives
red and yellow bell pepper strips
sour cream
fresh cilantro (optional)

Preheat oven to 350°. Wrap tortillas in foil and heat in oven for about 10 minutes. Scramble eggs and when cooked, place in a serving dish. Make fajitas by filling warmed tortilla with eggs and toppings of your choice.

Cantaloupe Wedge with Fruit Topping

1 cantaloupe wedge
strawberries, cubed
kiwi, cubed
pineapple, cubed
lime

Combine all ingredients except cantaloupe together in a small bowl. Add 1 tsp. corn syrup and a squeeze of lime. Spoon on top of cantaloupe wedge and serve.

Carrot Muffins

(makes 60 small muffins)

1 1/2 cups all-purpose flour
1/2 tsp. baking powder
1 tsp. ground cinnamon
1 tsp. ground nutmeg
1/2 tsp. salt
1/2 tsp. baking soda
2/3 cup vegetable oil
1 cup sugar
2 eggs, beaten
1 cup grated carrots
3/4 cup chopped walnuts

Preheat oven to 350°. Grease muffin tins. Sift together the dry ingredients and set aside. In a large bowl, combine the oil, sugar and eggs and mix by hand until blended. Add the dry ingredients into the oil, sugar, egg mixture. Mix well. Add the grated carrots and chopped nuts and stir.

Carefully spoon the batter into the muffin tins and bake for 20 minutes. Muffins are done when a toothpick inserted into the center comes out clean. Remove from tins to cool on a wire rack.

Cheddar Cornmeal Waffles with Salsa

(serves 4-5)

3 large eggs
1 3/4 cups buttermilk or soy milk
2 tbs. vegetable oil
1 cup all purpose flour
2 1/2 tsp. baking powder
1/4 tsp. baking soda
1 tsp. salt
1 tbs. sugar
1 cup fine cornmeal
1/2 cup shredded cheddar or soy cheese, for garnish
1/2 cup canned corn kernels, rinsed and drained
hot pepper sauce, to taste
1 ripe avocado, diced for garnish

Spray waffle iron with cooking spray. Preheat waffle iron. Beat eggs well, stirring in milk and oil. In a separate bowl, sift together the dry ingredients (flour, baking powder, baking soda, salt and sugar). Stir into the egg mixture, then add cornmeal, cheese, kernels and hot sauce. Bake waffles in the iron. When cooked, transfer to a serving platter.

Salsa topping for waffles:

1 cup thinly sliced black olives (pitted)
1/2 cup canned corn kernels, rinsed and drained
1 cup salsa
1 cup canned black beans, rinsed and drained

Combine all ingredients in a small saucepan. Bring to a boil over medium heat. Cook for 5 minutes until mixture is slightly reduced. Top waffles with salsa mixture and garnish with cheese and avocado.

Cheese Blintzes

(serves 8)

1 cup fat-free cottage cheese
4 oz. tub-style light cream cheese
1/4 cup sugar
1 tsp. vanilla extract
1 cup all-purpose flour
1 1/2 cups skim milk
1 1/2 tbs. vegetable oil
1 1/2 tsp. vanilla extract
1/4 tsp. salt
3 large eggs
cooking spray
2 cups fresh berries (blueberries, raspberries)
2 tsp. powdered sugar

In a blender, process cottage cheese until smooth. Add cream cheese, sugar, 1 teaspoon vanilla and process again until smooth. Pour into a bowl, cover and chill. Combine milk, oil, vanilla, salt and eggs and add to the flour. Stir with whisk until smooth. Cover and chill 2 hours. On medium-high heat, place a 10" crepe pan (non-stick skillet may be used), coated with cooking spray. Remove from heat. Pour 3 tbs. batter in pan and immediately tilt pan in all directions to cover skillet with a thin coating. Cook about 1 minute. Lift edges to test for doneness. When pancake is lightly brown and can be shaken loose, turn crepe over and cook approx. 30 seconds. Place on a towel to cool. Continue until all batter is used. Separate with a paper towel or waxed paper. Place 3 tablespoons of cottage cheese mixture in the center of each crepe. Fold over to form a rectangle. Place each crepe, seam side down on a baking sheet covered with plastic wrap. Chill in refrigerator. Coat a non-stick skillet with cooking spray and place over medium heat. Place 4 blintzes, seam side down in the skillet, cook for 2 minutes, turn and cook for 2 additional minutes. Repeat with the remaining crepes. Serve with warm berries over top and sprinkle with powdered sugar.

Cottage Cheese Pancakes

(serves 4)

1 large egg
1/8 cup cottage cheese
1/8 cup unbleached all-purpose flour
1 1/2 tbs. sugar
1 tbs. butter

In a mixing bowl, combine all of the ingredients except the butter. Stir together with a fork. Melt butter in a nonstick pan over medium heat. When the butter is hot but not brown, drop the batter by tablespoons into the hot pan. Cook for 3 minutes or until lightly browned. Flip pancakes and lightly brown the other side. Serve with yogurt, apple sauce or sour cream. They are also good with cinnamon sugar.

Cranberry Bread

(makes 1 loaf)
1/3 cup chopped nuts
1 3/4 cups (about 6 oz.) raw cranberries
1 orange and its juice, plus more juice to make 3/4 cup
2 cups flour
1 cup sugar
2 tsp. baking powder
1/2 tsp. baking soda
3/4 tsp. salt
1/4 cup vegetable oil
1 egg

Preheat oven to 350°. Grease a 9" x 5" loaf pan. Rinse cranberries and drain well. In a food processor fitted with a coarse blade, chop berries, but avoid pureeing. Set aside. Wash and dry the orange. Grate the colored part leaving the white bitter part. You should get about 2-3 teaspoons. Squeeze the juice into a measuring cup adding enough extra orange juice to give 3/4 cup total. Set aside. In a large mixing bowl, sift together the flour, sugar, baking powder, baking soda and salt. Stir in the chopped nuts and chopped cranberries and grated orange rind. Stir in the oil, egg and orange juice. Combine this mixture with the flour-cranberry mixture. Pour batter into prepared loaf pan and bake for 1 hour or until toothpick inserted into the middle comes out clean. Cool in the pan for 30 minutes and then out of the pan on a wire rack until completely cooled.

Cream Cheese and Salsa Wrap

(serves 2)

2 flour tortillas
4 tbs. cream cheese
2 tbs. salsa

Spread 2 tablespoons of cream cheese on one side of each tortilla.
Spread 1 tablespoon of salsa over cream cheese and roll up into a wrap.

Energy Muffins

(makes 12 muffins)

1 cup non-fat vanilla yogurt
1/2 cup skim milk
1 cup rolled oats
1/2 cup wheat germ
1/4 cup crushed pineapple, drained
1/4 cup sugar
3/4 cup brown sugar
1/4 cup egg substitute
1 cup whole wheat flour
2 tsp. baking powder
3/4 tsp. cinnamon
1 cup shredded zucchini
1/2 cup raisins
cinnamon-sugar (optional)

Preheat oven to 325°. Spray muffin tin with cooking spray. In a medium bowl, mix together yogurt, skim milk and oats. Cover with plastic wrap and set aside for 30 minutes until the oats soften. In a large bowl combine the wheat germ, pineapple, white and brown sugar, egg substitute, flour, baking powder, cinnamon, zucchini and raisins. Add the softened oat mixture to the large bowl of ingredients and blend well. Fill muffin cups 3/4 full and bake for 25-30 minutes. When a toothpick inserted into the middle of the muffins comes out clean, muffins are done. Sprinkle with cinnamon-sugar if desired.

Hole in One Eggs

(serves 1)

1 slice bread
butter
1 egg

Melt butter in a small skillet. Make a hole in the slice of bread about the size of the egg yoke. Crack egg in pan making sure not to break yolk. Place bread in pan with hole over yolk. Cook for 2 minutes on medium heat. Flip over and cook for another minute or two. Remove from pan and serve.

Homemade Trail Mix

2 cups granola or crunchy whole-grain cereal
1/3 cup raisins
1/3 cup chopped dates

Mix and eat.

Lemon-Poppy Seed Loaf

(makes 1 loaf)

1/2 cup butter, softened
1 cup sugar
2 eggs
1 tsp. grated lemon peel
1 1/2 cups all-purpose flour
1 tsp. baking powder
1/2 tsp. salt
1/3 cup milk
2 tbs. poppy seeds

Glaze:
juice of 1 lemon
1/2 cup Confectioners' sugar

Preheat oven to 350°. Grease a 9" x 5" loaf pan. In a large mixing bowl, beat the butter and sugar together. Beat in the remaining ingredients in the order listed. Pour the batter into the prepared loaf pan and bake for 55 minutes or until toothpick inserted into middle of the loaf comes out clean. Cool loaf in pan for 15 minutes, then turn onto a wire rack to continue cooling.
Make the lemon glaze by combining the lemon juice and Confectioners' sugar. Prick the loaf with a fork and pour the glaze over the top. Place a plate underneath the cooling rack to catch the glaze drips.

Microwaved Baked Apples

(serves 4)

4 Rome Beauty apples,
(about 2 lbs., cored and peeled halfway down from the stem)
1/2 cup orange juice or apple juice
1/2 tsp. ground cinnamon
grated nutmeg

Place cored and peeled apples in a microwave-safe dish with a lid. Evenly pour juice over apples. Sprinkle with cinnamon and nutmeg. Cover and microwave on high for 9 minutes.

(For one apple, prepare as above but microwave for 2-3 minutes.)

Pasta Frittata

(serves 4)

2 tsp. vegetable oil
1 cup chopped broccoli florets
1/2 cup diced carrots
1/2 cup frozen green peas, thawed
1 cup hot cooked angel hair pasta (2 oz. uncooked)
4 large eggs, lightly beaten
2 large egg whites, lightly beaten
1/8 tsp. salt
1/8 tsp. pepper
1/2 cup shredded cheddar cheese
1 cup tomato sauce

Heat oil in a large non-stick skillet on medium heat. Add broccoli, carrots and thawed peas and sauté for about 8 minutes. Stir in cooked pasta and cook for 1 minute. Whisk together in a large bowl eggs, egg whites, salt and pepper. Stir egg mixture into skillet with pasta and vegetables. Cook 5 minutes. Sprinkle with shredded cheese. Wrap the handle of the skillet with foil and broil for about 4 minutes until frittata is set. Remove from oven and slice into wedges. Serve with tomato sauce.

Pears with Maple Yogurt

1 tsp. maple syrup
yogurt (vanilla or plain)
pear
dried cranberries

Stir maple syrup into yogurt. Cut pear into wedges. Spoon yogurt on top of pear and sprinkle with dried cranberries.

Popcorn Balls

(makes 14)

8 cups popped popcorn
1 cup roasted peanuts
1 cup raisins
1/2 cup roasted sunflower seeds
2 tbs. honey crunch wheat germ
2 tbs. butter or margarine
2 tbs. peanut butter
1 (10 oz.) package marshmallows

In a shallow roasting pan, combine popcorn, peanuts, raisins, sunflower seeds and wheat germ. In a microwave-safe bowl, combine butter or margarine and peanut butter. Microwave uncovered for 1 minute on high. Add marshmallows and heat for another minute. Stir mixture and heat for 1 minute longer. Pour marshmallow mixture into roasting pan of popcorn mixture and stir. Rub hands lightly with vegetable oil. Use hands to form fourteen 3" wide balls. Let sit for 5 minutes. Wrap in waxed paper and store in cool area.

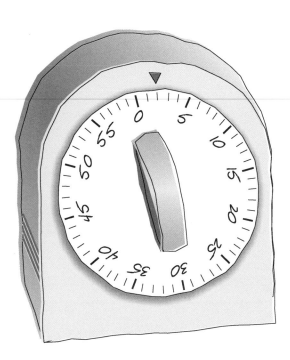

Puffed Pancake

(serves 2-4)

3 tbs. unsalted butter
2 large eggs, beaten
1/2 cup unbleached all-purpose flour
1/2 cup milk
2 tsp. sugar
pinch each of salt, nutmeg, and Confectioners' sugar
juice of 1/2 lemon

Preheat oven to 425°. Place butter in a 9" pie plate and put in oven to melt. This should take about 5 minutes. Watch to make sure it does not burn. In a medium bowl, whisk together the eggs, flour, milk, sugar, salt and nutmeg. When the butter has melted in the hot pie plate, pour in mixture and bake in oven for 20 minutes or until pancake has puffed up and become slightly brown. When pancake is cooked, it will look like a cushion with melted butter floating in the center. Remove from oven and sprinkle with sugar and lemon juice. Slice into wedges and serve immediately.

Pumpkin Muffins (Bread)

4 cups flour
3 cups sugar
2 tsp. baking soda
1 1/2 tsp. salt
1 tsp. baking powder
1 cup vegetable oil
2/3 cup water
4 eggs, beaten
1 1/2 cans pumpkin
1 tsp. cinnamon
1 tsp. allspice
1 tsp. ginger
1 tsp. nutmeg

Preheat oven to 350°. Place all dry ingredients in a bowl and make a well. Add oil, water, eggs and pumpkin. Mix, but do not beat. Grease and flour pans (muffin tins or loaf pan). Pour batter in pans. Place in oven for 20 minutes for muffins or 1 hour for loaf. Insert a toothpick into center. If it comes out clean, the muffins are done. Cool in pans for 15 minutes, and then out of pans on a wire rack.

Vegetable Puff with Asiago Cheese

(serves 4)

2 tbs. olive oil
1 cup chopped red onion
1 red pepper, chopped
1 medium zucchini, chopped
2 cups torn spinach leaves
3 large eggs
6 egg whites
1/2 tsp. salt
1/4 tsp. peppers
1 oz. shaved Asiago cheese
1 cup chopped seeded tomatoes
1 tbs. chopped fresh basil

Preheat broiler. Heat oil in a large non-stick skillet over medium-high heat. Combine onion and bell pepper and sauté approx. 8-10 minutes until lightly browned. Add zucchini and cook until soft. Add spinach and continue to cook until wilted. Season with salt and pepper. In a medium bowl, whisk eggs, egg whites, salt and pepper. Pour mixture over vegetables in skillet. Stir to combine all, reduce heat and cook until eggs are set (do not stir) on bottom and sides. Sprinkle cheese over eggs and broil until cheese melts. Garnish with tomatoes and basil. Can be served at room temperature. Artichoke hearts, roasted potatoes, broccoli or asparagus may also be added.

Zucchini Bread

(makes 1 loaf)

2 cups grated zucchini (about 1/2 lb.)
2 cups flour
1 cup sugar
1 tsp. baking powder
1/2 tsp. baking soda
1/2 tsp. ground cinnamon
1/2 tsp. salt
2 eggs
1/2 cup vegetable oil
1/2 cup water
1/2 tsp. vanilla

Wash and coarsely grate the zucchini; this should measure about 2 cups. Preheat oven to 350°. Grease a 9" x 5" loaf pan. Sift the dry ingredients together into a large bowl. Stir in the grated zucchini. In a small bowl, mix the eggs, oil, water and vanilla together. Pour into the large bowl of dry ingredients and stir just to combine. Pour batter into the prepared loaf pan. Bake for about 1 to 1 1/4 hours. Let cool in the pan.

Pasta, Pizza, Beans and Grains

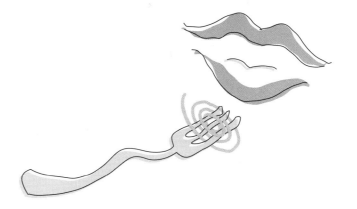

Baked Burritos

(serves 5)

2 (15 oz.) cans pinto beans, drained
1 (8 oz.) can tomato sauce
1/2 cup mild picante sauce
1 tsp. chili powder
3/4 cup grated sharp cheddar cheese
3/4 cup grated part-skim mozzarella cheese
10 (6") flour tortillas
2/3 cup mild picante sauce (optional)
1/2 cup sour cream (optional)

Preheat oven to 375°. In a food processor, combine beans, tomato sauce, picante sauce and chili powder. Process briefly until beans are almost puréed. In a small bowl combine the cheddar and mozzarella cheeses and set aside. To make the burritos, lay a tortilla out and put 1/3 cup of the bean mixture down the center in a line. Sprinkle with 2 tablespoons of the cheese mixture. Roll up and lay in a flat rectangular baking dish sprayed with non-stick cooking spray. Continue making burritos until all of the tortillas are used and the baking dish is filled. Sprinkle a little more cheese on top and bake uncovered for 11-14 minutes until hot. Top if desired with extra picante sauce and sour cream.

Black Beans and Rice

(serves 4)

1 (15 oz.) can black beans, undrained
1 (10 oz.) can diced tomatoes with green chilis (mild)
1/4 cup water
2 cups instant rice

In a medium saucepan, combine beans, tomatoes and water. Cover and bring to a boil on medium-high heat. Stir in rice. Cover, remove from heat and let stand for 5 minutes before serving.

Couscous Salad with Beans and Greens

(serves 4)

salt
1 1/3 cups couscous
1 1/2 tbs. lemon juice
pepper
4 tbs. extra-virgin olive oil
1/2 lb. asparagus, tough ends removed, cut into 1 1/2" pieces
1 (15 oz.) can cannellini or great northern beans, drained and rinsed
1 medium cucumber, peeled, seeded and diced
2 tbs. fresh basil minced

Boil 2 cups of water in a medium saucepan. Stir in 1 teaspoon salt and couscous. Remove pan from heat, cover and set aside for 5 minutes. In a large bowl, whisk together lemon juice, salt and pepper. Whisk in oil until smooth. Remove lid from pan and fluff couscous with a fork. Place couscous in a large bowl with the dressing and toss to coat evenly. Set aside to cool to room temperature. In a medium saucepan, bring 1 quart of water to boil. Add asparagus and cook about 2 minutes until tender. Drain and rinse asparagus under cold running water. Drain thoroughly. To the room temperature couscous, add asparagus, beans, cucumber and basil. Mix well. Serve at room temperature or chilled. Couscous will last up to 2 days. Note: you can use steamed spinach or mustard greens instead of asparagus for a change.

Homemade Fried Rice

2 cups short-grain brown rice
4 tbs. canola or olive oil
4 large eggs, lightly beaten
1 small red onion, chopped
1 small carrot, minced
1/2 cup frozen peas, thawed
4 scallions, finely chopped
1 tsp. salt
1/2 cup chopped fresh basil leaves

Combine rice and 4 cups of lightly salted water in a large saucepan. Bring to boil. Reduce heat to low, cover and simmer for 25-30 minutes or until all of the water is absorbed. In a large skillet, heat 2 tablespoons of the oil over medium-high heat. Add the eggs and scramble them until cooked through. Remove from skillet and set aside. Heat the remaining oil in the skillet and sauté the onions and carrots for about 2 minutes until onions are golden. Add the thawed peas and chopped scallions and cook for 2 more minutes. Stir in the salt, cooked rice and eggs. Toss and top with chopped basil. Serve.

Mac and Cheese

(serves 6)

2 1/2 cups milk
2 cups uncooked elbow macaroni
1 tbs. butter
3 tbs. all purpose flour
3/4 tsp. salt
1/2 tsp. dry mustard
2 cups plus 1/2 cup shredded sharp cheddar cheese

Preheat oven to 375°. Cook elbow macaroni according to package directions. While macaroni is cooking, heat milk and butter in a large saucepan over medium heat. Gradually whisk in flour, salt and dry mustard. Simmer uncovered for 1 minute, whisking occasionally. Remove from heat and stir in 2 cups of shredded cheddar cheese until melted. Drain cooked macaroni, add to cheese mixture and stir. Transfer mixture to a 9" square baking dish and bake uncovered for about 20 minutes until hot and bubbly. Top with the remaining cheese and let stand for five minutes before serving.

Make Your Own Pizza - Mexican

1 (10 oz.) store-bought thin pizza crust
1 (16 oz.) can vegetarian refried beans
1 cup Mexican-blend shredded cheese
shredded lettuce
chopped tomatoes
mild taco sauce

Preheat oven to 425°. Place pizza crust on a baking sheet. Spread refried beans over crust. Sprinkle cheese on top. Bake for 8-10 minutes until cheese melts and crust is crisp. Take out of oven and top with shredded lettuce, chopped tomatoes and taco sauce. Slice and enjoy.

Make Your Own Pizza - Primavera

1 (10 oz.) store-bought thin pizza crust
1/2 cup broccoli florets
1/2 cup sliced zucchini or yellow squash
1/2 cup shelled fresh green peas
olive oil
1/2 cup shredded mozzarella cheese
1/2 cup shredded cheddar cheese
1/2 cup sliced cherry tomatoes
2 green onions chopped
3 tbs. grated Parmesan cheese

Steam broccoli florets until crisp-tender. Immerse immediately in ice water to stop cooking process. Repeat with zucchini or yellow squash and green peas. Drain well and reserve.

Preheat oven to 425°. Place pizza crust on a baking sheet. Brush crust with a bit of olive oil and sprinkle with the shredded cheeses. Arrange the steamed vegetables and tomatoes on top of the cheese. Top with chopped green onions and drizzle olive oil evenly on top. Bake for 8-10 minutes until cheese melts and crust is crisp. Take out of oven and sprinkle with Parmesan cheese. Slice and enjoy.

Panzanella with White Beans and Goat Cheese

(serves 4 as a main course)

5 cups cubed day-old bread (country, sourdough, Italian)
1 (15 oz.) can white beans (great northern or cannellini)
4 oz. goat cheese, crumbled
3 tomatoes, chopped
1 bunch arugula or watercress, chopped
1/2 cup oil-cured olives, pitted and chopped
1/2 cup extra-virgin olive oil
1/4 cup red wine vinegar
1/4 cup minced parsley
1/4 tsp. salt

Note: If you don't have day-old bread, you can dry the bread cubes in a 350° oven on a cookie sheet until lightly browned. This should take about 15 minutes.

In a large bowl, whisk together the olive oil, vinegar, parsley and salt. Add the bread cubes and other ingredients and toss. Allow bread to absorb the liquid briefly before serving.

Pasta with Artichoke Hearts and Feta Cheese

(serves 4)

8 oz. uncooked pasta (spaghetti, linguini or shapes)
6 oz. jar marinated artichoke hearts
1/4 lb. crumbled feta cheese
1/4 cup chopped parsley
2 tbs. Parmesan cheese, grated
salt and pepper

Cook pasta according to package instructions. While pasta is cooking, chop artichoke hearts, reserving liquid. In a small bowl, combine artichokes and reserved liquid with feta cheese. When pasta is cooked, drain and top with artichoke-feta cheese mixture, parsley and Parmesan cheese. Toss well. Season with salt and pepper to taste.

Pasta with Tomatoes and Olives

(serves 8)

12 oz. radiator pasta (ruffles)
16 oz. Kalamata olives, pitted and sliced
1 (28 oz.) can diced tomatoes, drained
handful of fresh basil leaves, thinly sliced
3 tbs. olive oil
Parmesan cheese for garnish

Cook pasta according to directions, drain. Meanwhile, combine olives, tomatoes, basil and oil. Mix well. Spoon over pasta and serve hot or at room temperature. Top with grated Parmesan cheese if desired.

Pierogies Pesto

(serves 4)

1 (16.9 oz.) package potato & onion, or potato & cheddar pierogies
1 lb. fresh asparagus, trimmed and cut into 1" pieces
1/2 cup prepared pesto sauce
4 oz. smoked ham, cut into 1/4" strips (about 1 cup)
2 tbs. toasted pine nuts
fresh basil

Boil pierogies, adding asparagus during the last 2 minutes. Drain and reserve 1/4 cup of water. In the same saucepan, combine pesto, ham and reserved water. Heat until hot. Stir in pierogies. Garnish with pine nuts and fresh basil.

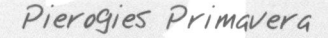
Pierogies Primavera

A change from Pasta Primavera! (serves 12)

3 (16.9 oz.) packages potato & onion or potato & cheddar pierogies
1 1/2 cups broccoli florets
3/4 cup thinly sliced zucchini
3/4 cup thinly sliced yellow squash
2 cups green and/or red pepper, cut into thin strips
3/4 cup thinly sliced carrots
1 1/2 cups thinly sliced mushrooms
1 cup bottled Italian dressing
1/4 cup thinly sliced red onion
2 tbs. chopped parsley

Cook pierogies according to package instructions. Boil water in a large pot and add broccoli, zucchini, squash, peppers, carrots and mushrooms. Cook vegetables about 20 seconds until just crisp-tender. Drain. In a large bowl of ice water, combine the cooked pierogies and the vegetables until cold, about 2 minutes. Drain. In a large mixing bowl, combine the pierogies and vegetables with Italian dressing, onion and chopped parsley. Chill at least 1 hour before serving.

Tomato-Spinach Risotto

(serves 4 main courses or 8 side servings)

5 cups reduced-sodium canned chicken broth
1 tbs. olive oil
1/2 cup chopped onion
1 1/2 cups uncooked arborio rice
1/3 cup dry white wine
1 (10 oz.) package frozen chopped spinach,
thawed and squeezed to remove water
1 (14 1/2 oz.) can diced tomatoes, drained
1/3 cup (1 1/2 oz.) grated Parmesan cheese
1/2 tsp. salt
1/8 tsp. pepper

In a medium saucepan, simmer chicken broth; do not boil. Keep warm over low heat. Heat oil in a large skillet on medium heat. Add chopped onion and cook for about 4 minutes until soft. Add rice to onions and stir for 1 minute constantly. Add wine and continue cooking and stirring until wine is absorbed, about 1 minute. Add chicken broth, 1/2 cup at a time, stirring constantly until each portion is absorbed before adding the next. The rice mixture should continually be at a gentle simmer. Continue adding broth and stirring until all of the broth is absorbed, about 25 minutes. Add spinach, tomatoes, cheese and salt and pepper to taste. Stir and serve.

Vegetable Lasagna

(serves 8)

1/4 cup olive oil
2 large onions, thinly sliced
3 cloves garlic, minced
1 lb. mushrooms, sliced
2 yellow bell peppers, thinly sl
1 (28 oz.) can crushed tomato
1/4 cup flat leaf parsley, mince
1 tsp. salt
1/2 tsp. pepper
18 dried lasagna noodles,
cooked according to package directions
1 lb. mozzarella cheese, shredded

Heat oil in a large saucepan. Add onions and sauté for about 10 minutes until onions are soft and translucent. Stir in garlic and sliced mushrooms. Continue cooking until mushrooms are soft, about 5 minutes. Add peppers and continue cooking for 3 more minutes. Stir in the tomatoes, parsley, salt and pepper. Simmer sauce for 10 minutes until it thickens.

Preheat oven to 400°. Grease a 13" x 9" x 2" baking dish. Spread 3-4 tablespoons of sauce on bottom of baking dish. Line the dish with a layer of cooked pasta. Sprinkle some of the cheese on top. Add another layer of pasta, tomato-vegetable sauce and cheese. Repeat 5 more times. Bake for 20-25 minutes until cheese turns golden brown. Remove from oven and let rest for 5 minutes before cutting into squares.

Poultry

Baked Breaded Chicken

(serves 4)
1 (3 lb.) chicken cut into 8 pieces
1/2 cup (1 stick) butter, melted
1 cup dry bread crumbs
1/2 cup grated Parmesan cheese
1/4 cup chopped parsley
1 garlic clove, minced
1 tsp. salt
1/4 tsp. pepper

Preheat oven to 375°. In a mixing bowl, combine the bread crumbs, cheese, parsley, garlic, salt and pepper. Melt butter and pour into another bowl. Dip chicken pieces in melted butter and then bread crumb mixture. Arrange in a shallow roasting pan or baking dish lined with foil for easy clean-up. Drizzle any remaining butter and bread crumbs. Bake uncovered for 30-45 minutes.

Capered Chicken Cutlets

(serves 4)
2 lbs. chicken breast cutlets
salt and pepper
2 tbs. olive oil
4 tbs. unsalted butter
1/4 cup capers

Season cutlets with salt and pepper. Heat olive oil in a large skillet over high heat and add chicken. Sauté for about 2 minutes on each side until browned and cooked through. Remove to a serving platter. Add butter to pan and melt. Cook until barely colored. Add capers to pan and cook another 15 seconds. Pour over chicken and serve.

Chicken and Artichokes

1 (6 oz.) jar marinated artichoke hearts, drained (save marinade)
3 tbs. canned, diced tomatoes with jalapenos
4 boneless, skinless chicken breast halves, trimmed
salt and pepper

Finely chop artichoke hearts. Coarsely chop tomatoes. Combine in a bowl with 1 tablespoon of artichoke marinade. Season to taste with salt and pepper. Flatten chicken breasts between plastic wrap to 1/2" thickness. Brush with artichoke marinade. Grill or broil 4" from heat for about 2 to 3 minutes on each side. Top chicken with artichoke-tomato salsa to serve.

Chicken Cutlets with Smoked Turkey and Fontina

2 split boneless, skinless chicken breasts
salt and pepper to taste
olive oil
4 slices smoked turkey
4 slices Italian fontina cheese

Preheat oven to 400°. Rub chicken with olive oil, salt and pepper. Flatten between plastic wrap to about 1/4" thickness. Place 1 slice of turkey and 1 slice of cheese on each breast half and fold chicken over top. Wrap in foil and bake for 15 minutes.

Chicken Fajitas

8 (6") flour tortillas
1 small onion, sliced
2 cloves garlic, minced
1 red or green bell pepper, sliced
2 tbs. vegetable oil
1 lb. chicken tenders
1/2 cup salsa
2 cups shredded lettuce
1/4 cup low-fat sour cream

Preheat oven to 300°. Wrap tortillas in foil and place in oven for 10 minutes or until heated through. Heat 1 tablespoon vegetable oil in a large skillet. Add onions and sauté for 2 minutes until translucent. Add garlic and bell pepper slices. Sauté for 1-2 more minutes until vegetables are tender-crisp. Remove from skillet. Heat the remaining 1 tablespoon of oil in the same skillet. Add chicken and stir-fry for 3-5 minutes or until chicken is no longer pink. Return veggies to skillet. Add salsa and cook until heated through. To serve, divide chicken mixture evenly among warmed tortillas. Top with shredded lettuce and a dollop of sour cream. Roll up tortillas and serve.

Crispy Dijon Chicken

(serves 6-8)

1 (3 lb.) chicken cut into 8 pieces
1/4 lb. (1 stick) unsalted butter, melted
2 tbs. vegetable oil
6 tbs. Dijon mustard
3 tbs. minced shallots
2 tbs. fresh thyme leaves
1 tsp. pepper
1/4 tsp. red pepper flakes
4 cups unseasoned bread crumbs

Preheat broiler. Broil chicken for 3 minutes on each side and remove. Set aside. Combine melted butter and oil. Set aside. In a medium bowl, blend the mustard, shallots, thyme, pepper and red pepper flakes. Stir in half of the butter and oil mixture. Mix thoroughly. Brush the prepared chicken with the mustard mixture and then coat completely with bread crumbs. Drizzle with the remaining melted butter and oil. Place pieces of chicken on a broiler pan and cook for 10-12 minutes under medium-high heat, turning chicken 2 to 3 times. Chicken is done when juices run clear.

Fast and Easy Chicken Chili

2 boneless, skinless chicken breasts, cut into cubes
2 cups flour
salt and pepper
2 tbs. corn oil
1 medium onion, chopped
1 clove garlic, minced
1 tbs. chili powder
1 tsp. cumin
3/4 cup chicken broth
1/4 cup crushed canned tomatoes
chopped cilantro for garnish, if desired

In a medium bowl, combine flour with salt and pepper. Roll chicken cubes in seasoned flour to coat. Shake off any excess flour. Heat oil in a large saucepan and brown chicken on all sides. Add the chopped onion and continue cooking until softened. Stir in garlic, chili powder and cumin. Add chicken broth and tomatoes. Simmer for about 7 minutes. Ladle into shallow bowls and garnish with chopped cilantro.

Lemon Chicken

(serves 6-8)

2 lbs. boneless, skinless chicken breasts
juice of 3 lemons, about 1 cup
2 cups unseasoned bread crumbs or flour
2 tsp. paprika
1 tsp. salt
1 tsp. pepper
1 tsp. olive oil
1 cup chicken broth
1/2 cup white wine
1 lemon, thinly sliced
1/4 cup brown sugar
1/4 cup chopped parsley

Marinate chicken breasts by placing them in a medium size non-metallic bowl. Pour fresh lemon juice on top and toss to coat. All of the chicken should be submerged in the juice. Let marinate at least 2 hours or overnight. Drain the chicken, pat dry with paper towels and set aside. Place bread crumbs in a large bowl and season with paprika, salt and pepper. Roll chicken breasts in bread crumbs and place on a clean tray. Once all of the chicken is breaded, heat 1 teaspoon olive oil in a large non-stick skillet. Add chicken and lightly fry on each side for about 2 minutes, just to color. Remove and place in a shallow rectangular baking dish. Continue to pan fry all of the chicken. Pour wine and chicken broth over the prepared chicken. Sprinkle with brown sugar and arrange lemon slices evenly on top. Bake covered in a preheated 350° oven for 30 minutes or until juices run clear. Remove from oven, sprinkle with chopped parsley and serve.

Oriental Chicken Kabobs

2 tbs. soy sauce
1 tbs. honey
1 tsp. ground ginger
1/2 tsp. dark sesame oil (oriental)
1 clove garlic, peeled and crushed
1 lb. boneless, skinless chicken breasts cut into 2" cubes
2/3 cup rice
1/4 tsp. salt
1 pint cherry tomatoes
1 green pepper cut into 1" squares
2 scallions, finely chopped

In a medium bowl, stir together soy sauce, honey, ginger, sesame oil and garlic. Toss chicken to coat thoroughly and let stand. Begin cooking rice: combine rice, 1 1/3 cups water and salt. Bring to a boil over high heat and reduce the heat to simmer in covered pan. Cook until rice is tender and water is absorbed (about 15 minutes).

Line broiler pan with foil. Alternate chicken, peppers and tomatoes on skewers. Broil about 5" from heat. Turn once after about 8 minutes. Continue cooking for another 8 minutes. (Can also be cooked on the grill.) Stir scallions into the rice. Place rice on plate, place skewered chicken on top.

Pasta Chicken Caesar Salad

3 cups cooked, shredded chicken
3 cups hot, cooked penne (about 6 oz. uncooked)
2 cups thinly sliced romaine lettuce
1 1/2 cups halved cherry tomatoes
1/2 cup thinly sliced basil
1/2 cup finely chopped green onions
1/3 cup Caesar dressing
1/4 cup finely chopped fresh parsley
4 oz. crumbled feta cheese
1 garlic clove, minced

Combine all ingredients. Toss well to coat.

Stuffed Chicken Breast

(serves 4)

2 boneless, skinless chicken breasts
1/2 cup chopped apple,
(golden delicious, granny smith, rome or winesap are good choices)
2 tbs. shredded cheddar cheese
1 tbs. seasoned bread crumbs
1 tbs. butter
1/4 cup dry white wine
1/4 cup water
1 tbs. water
1 1/2 tsp. cornstarch
1 tbs. chopped fresh parsley

In a small bowl, combine apple, cheese and bread crumbs. Set aside. Flatten chicken breasts between 2 sheets of waxed paper to 1/4" thickness. Spoon apple mixture evenly between chicken breasts and roll up. Secure each breast with toothpicks. Melt butter in a large skillet over medium heat. Brown stuffed chicken breasts on each side. Add wine and 1/4 cup water. Cover and simmer for 15-20 minutes until chicken is no longer pink. Remove chicken and place on a serving platter. Combine 1 tablespoon water with cornstarch. Stir into pan juices using a spoon to scrape any remaining chicken pieces. Simmer and stir until thickened. Pour gravy over the chicken and top with chopped parsley. Remove toothpicks and serve.

Turkey Enchilada

1/2 lb. ground turkey or beef
1 medium onion, chopped
1 garlic clove, minced
1 (16 oz.) can kidney beans
1 tsp. oregano
1 tbs. chili powder
2 tbs. seeded, diced green chilies (fresh or canned, drained)
1 (8 oz.) can tomato sauce
1/2 cup water
4 corn tortillas
1/2 cup shredded part-skim mozzarella cheese

Preheat oven to 375°. Sauté turkey or beef, onion and garlic in a non-stick fry pan until cooked through, stirring often. Drain any fat from pan. Combine in a saucepan beans, oregano, chili powder, chilies, tomato sauce and water. Bring to a boil and simmer for 5 minutes. Pour a small amount of the sauce to cover the bottom of a 6" casserole dish. Mix the rest of the sauce with the turkey or beef. Alternate layers of tortilla, meat mixture and shredded cheese. Bake in oven for 25-30 minutes until warmed through and cheese is melted.

Turkey Meatball Sub

1 (12 oz.) package frozen cooked turkey meatballs
1 1/2 cups tomato sauce
1/4 cup water
1/2-1 cup part-skim shredded mozzarella cheese
4 sub rolls

Heat broiler. In a large skillet on medium heat, place frozen turkey meatballs, tomato sauce and water until boiling. Reduce heat to medium-low and simmer, covered, 5 minutes or until meatballs are heated through. Stir occasionally. Meanwhile, place 4 sub rolls (sliced horizontally almost through), cut-side up, on a cookie sheet. Sprinkle with cheese. Broil 2-3 minutes or until cheese melts. Spoon meatballs and sauce on rolls. Cut sandwiches in half and serve.

Turkey Meatloaf

1 lb. ground turkey breast
1 egg white
1/2 cup oat bran
3 tbs. ketchup
1 tbs. Worcestershire sauce
1/2 tsp. Dijon mustard
1/2 green pepper, minced (or substitute red, orange or yellow)
3 slices onion, minced
2 tbs. chopped green olives (with pimento is fine)
1 large garlic clove, minced
1/4 tsp. each of sage, black pepper, celery salt

Preheat oven to 350°. Spray loaf pan with non-stick cooking spray. Mix all ingredients together and form into a loaf. Place in prepared pan. Bake for 1 1/4 hours. Do not over cook or it will dry out.

Serve with mushroom brown gravy, if desired.

Zippy Turkey Pesto

(makes 4 sandwiches)

1/3 cup prepared pesto
1/4 cup mayonnaise
1/4 cup roasted red pepper, drained and chopped
4 soft buns, split
4 lettuce leaves
1/2 lb. thinly sliced turkey breast
4 slices American or provolone cheese
4 tomato slices

Stir together pesto, mayonnaise and red pepper in a bowl. Mix well. Spread cut sides of buns with pesto mixture. Layer bottom half of each bun with lettuce leaf, 1/4 of the turkey, 1 slice cheese, 1 slice tomato and top half of bun.

Meat

Barbecued Short Ribs

(serves 4)

1/2 cup ketchup
1/4 cup fresh lemon juice
1/4 cup soy sauce
2 tsp. minced garlic
1 tsp. salt
4-5 lbs. short ribs, scored almost to the bone at 1/2" intervals
1/4 cup honey

In a medium bowl, combine the ketchup, lemon juice, soy sauce, garlic and salt. Stir. Arrange the ribs in a shallow dish. Pour half of the marinade over them and turn to coat the other side. Cover the ribs and refrigerate for 2 hours or up to 24 hours. Stir the honey in the remaining marinade. Cover and refrigerate. Heat grill. Place ribs in the center of the grill and cook for 10 minutes, turning once. Brush the ribs with the reserved marinade and continue to cook for 10 more minutes, turning occasionally and brushing frequently. The ribs should be shiny and dark brown when done. Serve ribs once split into serving-sized pieces.

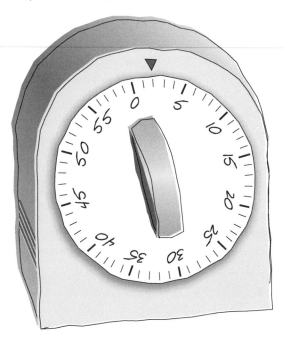

Beef Fajitas

(serves 4)

1/2 cup fresh lemon juice
1/3 cup olive oil
1/2 cup chopped cilantro
2 garlic cloves, minced
1 tsp. oregano
1/4 tsp. red pepper flakes
1/2 tsp. salt
1/4 tsp. black pepper
1 1/2 lbs. flank or skirt steak
2 red bell peppers, cut in half and seeded
8 (7") flour tortillas

Garnish:

1 small red onion, thinly sliced
1 cup salsa
1/2 cup sour cream
1/2 cup chopped black olives
2 cups shredded romaine lettuce

In a large bowl, whisk together lemon juice, oil, cilantro, garlic, oregano, pepper flakes, salt and pepper. Add steak and turn to coat on all sides. Add bell peppers and toss to coat. Cover bowl and refrigerate for at least 4 hours or up to 24 hours. Prepare grill. Remove steak from marinade and allow to reach room temperature. Place steak on center of grill rack and cook until well charred on both sides but pink in the center, 5-7 minutes per side. Transfer steak to cutting board. Place peppers on center of grill rack and cook until peppers are charred and softened on both sides, 3 minutes per side.

Stack the tortillas, wrap in foil and put on side of grill to warm. Turn occasionally. Arrange garnishes in bowls. Transfer peppers to cutting board. Cut steak and peppers into long, thin strips and arrange side by side on a serving platter. Put a tortilla on a plate and top with steak, peppers and any garnishes. Roll up tortilla to enclose the filling.

Far Eastern Steak Salad

Marinade:
juice and zest of 1 lime
1 tbs. grated fresh ginger
1 garlic clove, minced
1 scallion sliced into 1/4" rounds, only use white and light green parts

Salad:
12 oz. flank steak
fresh ground pepper
1 red bell pepper, julienned
2 carrots, peeled and julienned
1 head Napa cabbage, julienned (remove outer leaves)
1 papaya, peeled and cut into 2" pieces (remove seeds)
1/4 cup fresh cilantro leaves
1/4 cup fresh mint leaves
1 cup bean sprouts (optional)
2 tbs. chopped toasted peanuts

Combine all ingredients for marinade. Place steak in a shallow dish, cover with marinade on both sides. Refrigerate in marinade for 1 hour. Prepare salad ingredients and toss together. Refrigerate. Remove steak from refrigerator 30 minutes prior to cooking. Heat grill over medium-high heat. Season steak with black pepper. Sear steak until browned on the outside and cooked to desired doneness (5-6 minutes on each side for medium-rare). Let cool slightly and cut thin slices on the bias. Serve sliced steak over salad.

Hearty Pasta Saute

(serves 4)

8 oz. spaghetti or fusilli
2 tbs. olive oil
1 1/2 oz. Italian bread torn into small pieces (1 1/2 cups)
8 oz. uncooked Italian sweet or hot sausage,
(ground beef may be substituted)
2 medium green or red tomatoes, cut into wedges
1 medium red onion, chopped
1 medium green, red or yellow pepper, cut into bite-size pieces
1 (26 oz.) jar pasta sauce with olives

Cook pasta, drain. In a large skillet, heat oil over medium-high heat. Add torn bread pieces and cook for 2-3 minutes to toast. Remove from skillet. Remove casings from sausage and cook sausage with tomatoes, onion, and pepper over medium heat for 6-8 minutes or until vegetables are tender and sausage is browned. Drain fat and add pasta sauce. Stir until heated through. Serve sauce over pasta. Top with toasted bread.

Osso Buco

(serves 5-6)

3-4 lbs. veal shanks
salt and pepper
flour
1/4 cup vegetable oil
2 medium onions, chopped
3 stalks of celery, chopped
3 carrots, chopped
1 cup dry white wine
1 can of tomato paste
1 1/2 cups water
1 lb. of spaghetti
1 tbs. grated lemon rind
2 tbs. chopped parsley
1 clove garlic, minced

In a medium bowl, place flour for dredging. Season with salt and pepper. Roll shanks in flour and pat to remove any excess flour. Repeat for all shanks. Heat oil in a large soup pot and brown shanks on all sides. This should take about 2-3 minutes per side. Remove to platter. To the large pot, add the chopped onions, celery and carrots. Cook for 2-3 minutes and then add the wine, tomato paste and water. Bring to a boil. Return the veal shanks to the pot and cover. Cook over low heat for 1 1/2 hours until meat is tender. If the sauce has reduced too much, add a little water. In a separate pot, cook the spaghetti until done. Serve veal on top of spaghetti, sprinkled with combined lemon rind, parsley and garlic.

Squash and Chard Chili

(serves 6)

3/4 lb. lean ground beef
1 cup diced onion
1 cup sliced carrot
1 cup diced red bell pepper
2 garlic cloves, minced
1 (15 oz.) can black beans, drained and rinsed
2 (14.5 oz.) cans diced tomatoes
3 cups diced, peeled butternut squash (1/2" cubes)
3 cups water
1 1/2 tbs. chili powder, or to taste
1 tsp. cumin
1 tsp. oregano
1/2 tsp. salt
4 cups coarsely chopped Swiss chard leaves
6 tbs. (1 1/2 oz.) shredded, reduced-fat cheddar cheese

Crumble beef in a large soup pot over medium-high heat. Add onion, carrot and red pepper and cook, stirring occasionally, until meat is browned (about 5 minutes). Add the garlic, beans, tomatoes, squash, water, chili powder, cumin, oregano and salt; stir to combine. Bring to a boil, then reduce heat and simmer gently, stirring occasionally, until squash is tender (about 30 minutes). Stir in the Swiss chard; cover and cook 5 minutes. Uncover and simmer, stirring occasionally, an additional 10 minutes or until chard is tender. To serve, ladle into bowls and top with shredded cheese.

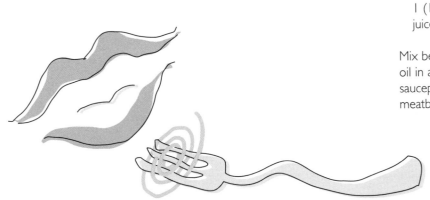

Standing Rib Roast

(serves 6-8)

1 (3-rib) standing rib roast (7-8 lbs.)
1 tbs. kosher salt
1 1/2 tsp. pepper

Remove meat from refrigerator and allow to come to room temperature for two hours before roasting. Preheat oven to 500°. Place the oven rack on the second lowest position. Put the roast in a roasting pan bone-side down. Season thickly with salt and pepper. Roast for 45 minutes. Without opening oven door, reduce the heat to 325° and roast for another 30 minutes. Increase the temperature to 450° and roast for another 15-30 minutes. The total cooking time should be between 1 1/2 to 1 3/4 hours. The internal temperature of meat should read 125°. Remove the roast from the oven and place on a cutting board. Cover tightly with aluminum foil and allow meat to rest for 20 minutes. Carve meat and serve.

Sweet and Sour Meatballs

(makes 50 small or 25 large meatballs)

2 lbs. ground beef
1 egg, slightly beaten
1 large onion, grated
salt to taste
oil
1 (12 oz.) bottle chili sauce
1 (10 oz.) jar grape jelly
juice of 1 lemon

Mix beef, egg, onion and salt and shape into small balls. Brown meatballs in oil in a skillet. Remove and drain on paper towels as done. In a medium saucepan, combine the chili sauce, grape jelly and lemon juice. Drop meatballs into sauce. Simmer until meatballs are cooked through.

Teriyaki London Broil

1 cup soy sauce
1/4 cup vegetable oil
1/4 cup apricot jam
4 tsp. cornstarch
1/4 tsp. black pepper
3 garlic cloves, peeled
2 lbs. top round, 1 1/4" thick
12 mushrooms, trimmed and wiped clean
24 cherry tomatoes

Prepare grill or preheat broiler. If broiling, line a rimmed baking sheet with foil. In a small saucepan, combine soy sauce, oil, apricot jam, cornstarch, pepper and whole garlic cloves. Stir to blend and bring to a boil over medium heat, stirring constantly. Remove from heat. Place steak on grill or on a baking sheet. Brush the steak with the sauce. Grill or broil the steak 4" from heat, turning once and brushing the second side with sauce (5-7 minutes for rare; 8-10 minutes per side for medium; 11-13 minutes for well done).

Dividing the mushrooms and tomatoes evenly, place them on skewers. About 4 minutes before the steak is done, brush vegetables with sauce and place on grill or broiler for 2 minutes. Turn, brush with sauce, and cook for 2 minutes. Allow steak to rest for 10 minutes before slicing. Cut across the grain, on the diagonal, into thin slices. Remove garlic from remaining sauce and bring to a boil. Serve steak and vegetables with sauce on the side.

Tiny Meatballs

1 lb. ground beef
1/2 cup seasoned bread crumbs
1 egg, beaten (lightly)
1/4 cup water
1/4 cup Parmesan cheese

Preheat oven to 400°. In a medium bowl, mix all ingredients together. Form into balls, arrange on baking sheet. Bake for 20 minutes. Serve on top of pasta or rice.

Turkey and Ham Focaccia

(makes 6 sandwiches)

1 (12 oz.) loaf focaccia bread (about 9"), sliced in half horizontally
1/2 cup cream cheese with chives and onion
24 fresh spinach leaves, stems removed
8 slices of deli turkey breast
6 slices of American cheese
8 slices of deli ham
6 slices of provolone cheese
2 medium tomatoes, thinly sliced

Spread both cut sides of bread halves with cream cheese. Layer bottom half with 1/2 of the spinach leaves, all of the turkey, American cheese, ham, provolone cheese, tomatoes and then the remaining spinach. Cover with top half of focaccia. Cut into 6 wedges. Secure each with toothpick.

Zesty Barbecue Pitas

1 tsp. butter
2 medium onion, sliced
1 cup barbecue sauce
12 oz. thinly sliced deli roast beef, cut into bite-sized pieces
1 (11 oz.) can whole kernel corn with red and green peppers, drained
6 (6") pita breads, cut in half, warmed
12 lettuce leaves
12 slices American cheese, cut in half diagonally

Melt butter in a large skillet until sizzling, add onions. Cook over medium-high heat, stirring occasionally, until softened (4-6 minutes). Add barbecue sauce, roast beef and corn. Continue cooking, stirring occasionally, until heated through (4-6 minutes). Fill each pita half with 1 lettuce leaf, 2 halves cheese and 1/3 cup beef mixture. Serve.

Seafood

Fresh Tuna Burgers

(serves 4)

1 lb. fresh raw tuna
1 tbs. water
salt and pepper
1/4 tsp. garlic powder (do not use fresh garlic)
2 tbs. olive oil
4 buns or bread of your choice

To make the tuna burgers, chop the tuna finely and mix with water, salt, pepper and garlic powder and form into 4 tightly packed patties. Coat with olive oil. Grill or broil for 4 minutes per side if you like a pink center, or longer for more well done. Serve on toasted buns topped with condiments of your choice.

Grilled Fresh Tuna Salad

(serves 4)

3 tbs. soy sauce
1/4 cup orange juice
2 tbs. rice wine vinegar
1 tbs. brown sugar
1 tbs. grated orange peel (optional)
1 garlic clove, minced
1/2 tsp. hot pepper sauce
1 lb. ahi or yellowfin tuna, about 1" thick,
(may substitute salmon or halibut)
8 red-skinned potatoes, halved
4 plum tomatoes, halved lengthwise
2 yellow or orange bell peppers, cored, seeded and cut into wedges
1 large red onion, sliced
2 heads romaine lettuce
1 bunch basil leaves
3 tbs. extra-virgin olive oil
juice of 1 lemon
salt and pepper

Make a marinade for tuna by combining the soy sauce, orange juice, vinegar, brown sugar, orange peel if desired, garlic and hot pepper sauce in a shallow dish. Add the tuna. Cover with plastic wrap and set aside for about 15 minutes. Light the grill or broiler. When it is hot, place tuna on grill or 6" beneath broiler.

Place potatoes, tomatoes, peppers and onion slices into marinade to coat. Place on grill or broiler pan, cut-side down. Close grill lid or oven door and cook for 7 minutes. Flip fish and vegetables. Discard marinade. Close lid or door again and cook fish and vegetables for another 7 minutes until tuna is cooked through and vegetables are tender. Arrange romaine lettuce and basil leaves on a serving platter. Toss with olive oil, lemon juice, salt and pepper. Top with grilled tuna and vegetables and serve.

Italian Tuna, White Bean and Escarole Salad

Toss canned tuna packed in oil with some canned white beans, a bunch of escarole leaves and oil and vinegar. Add some croutons for a little crunch if desired. Serve at room temperature or chilled.

Light Crab Cakes

1 lb. lump or backfin crabmeat picked over for cartilage
2 egg whites, beaten
1/2 cup dry bread crumbs
1 tbs. Worcestershire sauce
1 tbs. chopped parsley
1 tbs. baking powder
1 tbs. light mayonnaise
1 tsp. Old Bay seasoning
vegetable cooking spray

Combine all ingredients except cooking spray. Form into 4 patties. Cook in a non-stick pan sprayed with vegetable cooking spray over medium heat until golden brown.

Linguini with Shrimp Scampi

(serves 4)
salt
12 oz. linguini
1/4 cup olive oil
3 garlic cloves, minced
1 lb. medium shrimp, shelled and de-veined
1 lemon, zest finely grated, juice squeezed
1/2 tsp. pepper
1/2 cup fresh parsley, minced

Boil water in a large pot. Add salt and linguini. Cook until tender, about 8 minutes. stirring often. Drain pasta in a colander and set aside. Heat olive oil in a skillet. Add garlic and cook for 1 minute over medium heat. Stir often to make sure garlic does not burn. Add shrimp, lemon zest, salt and pepper and stir well. Add 1/4 cup of water and the lemon juice and simmer for 1 minute. Add parsley and continue simmering until the shrimp are cooked. This should be another 2 minutes or so. Place cooked linguini in a serving bowl and top with shrimp and its sauce. Toss well and serve Italian bread on the side.

Oven-Baked Fried Fish

(serves 4)
1/2 cup milk or 1 egg, beaten
1/4 tsp. tarragon
1/2 cup bread crumbs
1/2 tsp. paprika
1 tsp. grated Parmesan cheese
1/4 tsp. dry mustard
2 lbs. fish fillets (flounder, cod, sole)
lemon juice, to taste
chopped fresh parsley for garnish

Preheat oven to 475°. Lightly oil a baking sheet or shallow baking dish. In a large bowl, combine the milk or beaten egg with tarragon. In another large bowl, mix bread crumbs, paprika, Parmesan cheese and dry mustard. Dip each fish fillet into the milk or egg and then roll into the bread crumb mixture. Transfer to an oiled baking sheet or dish and bake for 7-10 minutes depending on thickness. Fillets should be golden brown and cooked through. Serve with a squeeze of fresh lemon juice and chopped parsley for garnish.

Pierogi Nicoise Salad

(serves 4)
1 (16.9 oz.) package potato & cheddar, or potato & onion pierogies
8 oz. fresh or 1 (9 oz.) package frozen green beans
1/3 cup bottled Caesar dressing
8 romaine lettuce leaves
1 tomato, sliced
4 hard-cooked eggs, halved
1 (6-7 oz.) can water-packed tuna, drained
1/4 cup pitted black olives, halved

Add pierogies to a large pot of boiling water. Return to a boil and stir occasionally until tender, about 3 minutes. Add green beans and cook until pierogies float to the surface, about 3 more minutes. Drain. In a large bowl, toss hot pierogies and beans with Caesar dressing. Allow to come to room temperature or chill. Place 2 lettuce leaves on each of 4 plates and arrange pierogies on top. Garnish with tomatoes, eggs, tuna and olives, dividing all ingredients evenly. Serve extra dressing on the side, along with anchovies and capers if desired.

Salmon Baked in Foil

(serves 4)
4 tbs. extra virgin olive oil
2 lbs. salmon fillet, cut into 4 pieces
12 cherry tomatoes, halved
salt and pepper
16 basil leaves

Cut 4 pieces of aluminum foil into 12" sheets. Each sheet will hold 1 piece of salmon. Smear the first sheet with 1/2 tbs. olive oil. Place salmon on top and layer with 6 tomato halves, salt and pepper, 4 basil leaves and another 1/2 tbs. olive oil. Seal the package by folding the foil over onto itself and crimping the edges tightly. Repeat this procedure with the other three packages. These may be made ahead of time and kept refrigerated for up to 24 hours.

Preheat oven to 500°. Lay salmon packages in a roasting pan. Cook 10-12 minutes for medium rare, and 15-20 minutes for medium. Let fish packages rest a few minutes and then open by cutting a slit along the top with a knife. Serve salmon on a plate with the garnishes and juices on top.

Salmon with Red Onions

(serves 4)

2 lbs. salmon fillet
1 large red onion, thinly sliced
2 tbs. olive oil
2 tbs. balsamic vinegar
1 tbs. honey
1 tbs. butter
salt and pepper

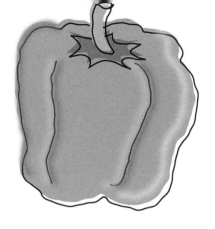

Preheat oven to 350°. Place salmon in a baking dish and rub with 1 tablespoon olive oil, salt and pepper. Bake in oven for 10 minutes. While salmon is baking, toss sliced onions with remaining 1 tbs. olive oil, vinegar, honey, salt and pepper in a bowl until well coated. Melt butter in a sauté pan and cook onion mixture until it starts to brown slightly and caramelize. Remove salmon from oven and top with caramelized onions. Put back in oven and bake for another 10 minutes and serve.

Scallops with Almonds

(serves 4)

1 lb. sea scallops
1/4 tsp. salt
1/4 tsp. pepper
1/2 cup bread crumbs
1 tbs. butter
1/2 cup slivered almonds
2 tbs. chopped parsley

Rinse scallops in cool water and pat dry. Season with salt and pepper and roll in bread crumbs. Melt butter in pan and sauté until cooked through and browned on each side. This should take about 8 minutes, depending on the size of the scallops. Remove from pan, top with slivered almonds and chopped parsley.

Shrimp and White Bean Salad

Toss canned white beans and cooked shrimp with lemon juice, minced garlic and fresh herbs of your choice. Serve on top of lettuce or on a crusty roll.

Shrimp Wrap with Corn Salsa

(serves 6-8)

1 lb. cooked salad shrimp
1/4 cup lime juice
2 tsp. olive oil
1/2 tsp. garlic powder
6-8 flour tortillas

Corn Salsa:
1 medium red onion, chopped
1 cup frozen corn kernels, thawed
1/2 cucumber, peeled, seeded and chopped
1/4 cup finely chopped cilantro
1/2 cup red bell pepper, chopped
2 jalapeno chilies, finely chopped (optional)
salt and pepper

Marinate shrimp in lime juice, olive oil and garlic powder for 30 minutes. While shrimp is marinating, combine the corn salsa ingredients. Drain shrimp from marinade. Make wraps using 1/4 cup shrimp in each tortilla. Roll up and top with salsa.

Spinach Salad with Shrimp

(serves 4)
Salad ingredients:
1 cup cooked salad shrimp
4 cups fresh spinach leaves
1 cup mushrooms, sliced
1 apple, chopped
1/4 cup red onion, chopped
1/4 cup grated carrot
1/4 cup raisins
1 (4 oz.) can mandarin oranges, drained

Dressing:
2 tbs. frozen orange juice concentrate
1 tbs. olive oil
1 tbs. water
1 tbs. white vinegar
1/8 tsp. dried tarragon
1/8 tsp. dried parsley
1/8 tsp. garlic powder
1/8 tsp. pepper

In a large bowl, combine all of the salad ingredients except the mandarin oranges. Mix dressing ingredients together and pour over salad. Toss. Top with mandarin oranges. Serve immediately. This salad can be made ahead of time. Pour on the dressing just before serving.

Teriyaki Grilled Salmon

(serves 4)

1 lb. salmon fillets, cut into 4 pieces
vegetable cooking spray
1/2 cup white wine
1/4 cup brown sugar
3 tbs. light soy sauce
3 cloves garlic, minced
1/2 tsp. ground ginger

Mix all ingredients except salmon and cooking spray in a shallow non-metallic dish. Reserve 3 tbs. of marinade. Place fish in marinade and let sit for 20 minutes, turning once. Remove fish and discard marinade. Coat salmon with vegetable cooking spray and grill or broil approximately 3 minutes. Turn and brush with reserved marinade. Cook for additional 4-5 minutes or until desired doneness.

Tuna Melt

(serves 8)

1 (6 oz.) can tuna, drained
1/4 cup mayonnaise
1/4 cup celery, finely chopped
1/4 cup reduced-fat cheddar cheese, shredded
1/8 tsp. garlic powder
1/8 tsp. pepper
1 (8 oz.) package refrigerated crescent rolls

Preheat oven to 375°. Combine tuna, mayonnaise, celery, cheese, garlic powder and pepper in a small bowl. Separate crescent roll dough into 8 triangles. Put 1 tablespoon of tuna mixture on a corner of each triangle and roll up. Bake on an ungreased cookie sheet for 13-16 minutes or until golden brown.

Vegetables

Antipasto Salad

(serves 8)

1 (6 oz.) can tuna in water, drained
1 (16 oz.) can garbanzo beans, drained
1 (16 oz.) can kidney beans, drained
1/2 cup chopped celery
1/2 small red onion, finely chopped
1/2 green pepper, seeded and chopped
1 large carrot, chopped
1 (10 oz.) can quartered artichoke hearts, rinsed and drained
8 cherry tomatoes, halved
3/4 cup Italian dressing
4 cups shredded romaine lettuce
2 tbs. chopped parsley, for garnish

Combine all ingredients except salad dressing, shredded lettuce and chopped parsley. Toss lightly. Add dressing and toss again. Chill for 30 minutes. To serve, place shredded romaine lettuce on individual plates and top with antipasto salad and lightly sprinkle with chopped parsley.

Broccoli in Creamy Balsamic Sauce

(serves 4)

1 head broccoli, trimmed and broken into large florets
2 tbs. balsamic vinegar
2 tbs. dry red wine
6 tbs. unsalted butter, cold and cut into cubes
salt and pepper

Cook broccoli until tender. Drain. In a saucepan, combine vinegar and wine and cook over medium-high heat until reduced by half. Take off heat and stir in cubed cold butter until creamy. Season with salt and pepper. Place broccoli in a serving dish and pour balsamic sauce on top and toss. Serve immediately.

Carrot Souffle

(serves 4)
3 cups cooked carrots
2/3 cup sugar
3 tbs. all-purpose flour
1 tsp. baking powder
1/2 cup butter (1 stick), melted
3 large eggs, beaten

Preheat oven to 400°. Mash cooked carrots and measure 3 cups. Put in a large bowl. Add sugar, flour, baking powder, melted butter and beaten eggs and mix. Pour into a greased, shallow casserole dish and bake covered with foil for 15 minutes. Reduce heat to 350° and bake uncovered for 45 minutes. Soufflé is finished when a toothpick inserted into the center comes out clean.

Coleslaw

(serves 8-10)
1/2 head red cabbage, finely shredded
1/2 head green cabbage, finely shredded
2 carrots, peeled and grated
1 small yellow onion, chopped
1 green bell pepper, seeded and cut into julienne strips
1/2 yellow bell pepper, seeded and cut into julienne strips
1/2 red bell pepper, seeded and cut into julienne strips
1 cup tarragon vinegar
3/4 cups canola oil
1/2 cup sugar
3/4 tbs. dry mustard
3/4 tbs. celery seeds
salt and pepper, to taste

In a large mixing bowl, combine the red and green cabbages, carrots, onions and peppers. In a medium saucepan, mix the vinegar, oil, sugar, mustard and celery seeds. Heat just to boiling and then lower heat and simmer for 1 minute. Pour mixture over the coleslaw and toss well. Season with salt and pepper. Place the coleslaw in a serving dish and refrigerate for several hours before serving.

Corn Pudding

(serves 6)
8-10 ears fresh corn, or 2 1/2 cups frozen corn kernels, thawed
1 egg
1/2 cup light cream
1/2 cup heavy or whipping cream
1 tbs. brown sugar
2 tbs. chopped chives
nutmeg
salt and pepper
1/2 cup, plus 3 tbs. crumbled Ritz crackers
4 tbs. (1/2 stick) unsalted butter, melted

Preheat oven to 350°. Butter a 6-8 cup casserole dish. Cut corn off the cob or measure 2 1/2 cups frozen corn, thawed. Set aside. In a large bowl, beat the egg, light cream, heavy cream and brown sugar just until blended. Stir in chives, pinch of nutmeg, salt and pepper and corn. In another bowl, toss 1/2 cup cracker crumbs with 3 tablespoons melted butter. Stir into corn mixture. Pour the corn mixture into the buttered casserole dish. Mix the remaining 3 tablespoons of cracker crumbs with the remaining 1 tablespoon of melted butter. Sprinkle the crumbs over the top of the pudding. Bake uncovered for approximately 50-60 minutes, until slightly firm and lightly golden brown.

Honey-Ginger Carrots

(serves 4)
6 large carrots, peeled
2 tbs. olive oil
1 tbs. grated fresh ginger
2 tbs. honey
1/2 tsp. kosher salt

Shred carrots using a food processor or a large grater. In a medium bowl, mix together the other ingredients. Place shredded carrots in the bowl. Toss to coat.

Skillet: Add all ingredients to a skillet and sauté over medium heat until carrots are tender-crisp.

Microwave: Place carrots on a microwave-safe plate. Cover and microwave on high for 3-5 minutes, or until carrots are tender-crisp.

Quick and Easy Ratatouille

(serves 6 as a side dish, or 4 as an entrée)
2 large zucchini squash
4 medium tomatoes
2 medium onions
2 green peppers
3 tbs. olive oil
2 cloves garlic, minced
salt and pepper
grated Parmesan cheese (optional)

Thinly slice onions and tomatoes. Core and seed peppers, cutting them into thin strips. Dice zucchini squash. Heat olive oil in a large skillet and sauté onions until translucent. Add squash, tomatoes and peppers. Simmer gently for about 10 minutes. Add garlic, salt and pepper. Cover and simmer for 10 more minutes. Serve hot, room temperature or cold. Sprinkle with Parmesan cheese if desired.

Roasted Asparagus with Cheese and Pine Nuts

(serves 6)
1 lb. fresh asparagus (white portion cut off)
2 tbs. olive oil
1/4 cup romano cheese, grated
1/4 cup pine nuts
salt and pepper
juice of 1 lemon

Set broiler to high heat. Place asparagus on a baking sheet and brush with olive oil on all sides. Sprinkle salt, cheese and pine nuts on top. Broil until cheese melts for about 4-5 minutes. Remove from broiler and add pepper and a squeeze of lemon. Serve immediately.

Roasted Potatoes Topped with Sun-Dried Tomato Pesto

(serves 8)

16 small red skinned potatoes, halved
1 cup sun-dried tomatoes (not oil-packed)
2 tbs. pine nuts
2 cloves garlic, minced
6 fresh basil leaves
2 tbs. olive oil
juice of 1 lemon
salt and pepper
2 tbs. fresh parsley or basil, chopped for garnish

Preheat oven to 450°. Coat baking sheet and brush potatoes with olive oil. Bake potato halves until tender, approximately 20 minutes. In a medium bowl, pour hot water over tomatoes and let stand for about 15 minutes until softened. Remove tomatoes with a slotted spoon, reserving liquid. Transfer tomatoes to a food processor or blender and add pine nuts, garlic and basil. Purée. Gradually add olive oil and 1/4 cup reserved tomato water, lemon juice, salt and pepper. Purée again. When potatoes are cooked, place in a bowl and toss pesto with hot potatoes. This pesto is also good tossed with pasta or rice, and it makes a great omelette filling.

Roasted Root Vegetables

(serves 8)

1 lb. carrots, peeled
1 lb. parsnips, peeled
1 large sweet potato, peeled
1 small butternut squash, peeled and seeded
3 tbs. olive oil
1 1/2 tsp. kosher salt
1/2 tsp. freshly ground pepper
2 tbs. flat-leaf parsley, minced

Preheat oven to 425°. Cut all vegetables into 1" cubes. Place in a single layer on two baking sheets. Drizzle with olive oil and sprinkle with salt and pepper. Toss to coat. Bake until all vegetables are tender, approximately 30-40 minutes. Using a spatula, turn once during cooking time. Sprinkle with parsley when cooking is complete and serve.

Spaghetti Squash Saute

(serves 6)

1 spaghetti squash
3 tbs. butter
3 cloves garlic, minced
2 tsp. minced shallots
3 tbs. minced parsley
salt and pepper

Preheat oven to 350°. Cut spaghetti squash in half lengthwise and remove seeds. Place squash in a shallow pan with water half way up the side of the squash. Bake for approximately 1-1 1/2 hours, until completely soft. Remove from oven and set aside until cool. Using a fork, scrape the meat out of the squash into a bowl. This should resemble spaghetti. At this point, squash can be refrigerated for 1-2 days if desired. Heat butter in a skillet and add shallots and garlic. Sauté for a few minutes until translucent. Add spaghetti squash and heat through. Add parsley, salt and pepper to taste. Serve.

Steamed Brussels Sprouts

(serves 4)

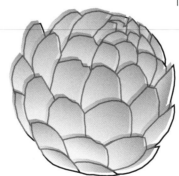

1 lb. Brussels sprouts
3 tbs. unsalted butter
1 tbs. poppy seeds
pinch of grated nutmeg
salt and pepper

Trim the ends of the Brussels sprouts and cut an X on the bottom of each. Steam sprouts in boiling water just until tender. Drain. Melt butter in a small saucepan or microwave butter in a medium bowl to melt. Add the poppy seeds, nutmeg, salt and pepper to taste. Place hot Brussels sprouts in a serving dish and pour the melted butter over top and toss. Serve immediately.

Sweet Potato and Apple Casserole

(serves 6)

2 large sweet potatoes
2 firm green apples
1 cup light brown sugar, firmly packed
1 tsp. allspice
3/4 cup butter (or margarine), melted
2 tbs. lemon juice
cinnamon
1/4 cup maple syrup or honey

Preheat oven to 350°. Wash and peel sweet potatoes. Cut into 1/4" slices. Wash and core apples. Slice into 1/4" slices. In a small saucepan, melt butter or margarine and gradually add brown sugar, allspice, syrup or honey and lemon juice. Stir and set aside. In a casserole dish, alternate layers of potatoes, apples and some of the syrup from saucepan, ending with potatoes. Sprinkle cinnamon on top layer and bake for 35 minutes until nicely browned.

RECIPE INDEX

RECIPE INDEX

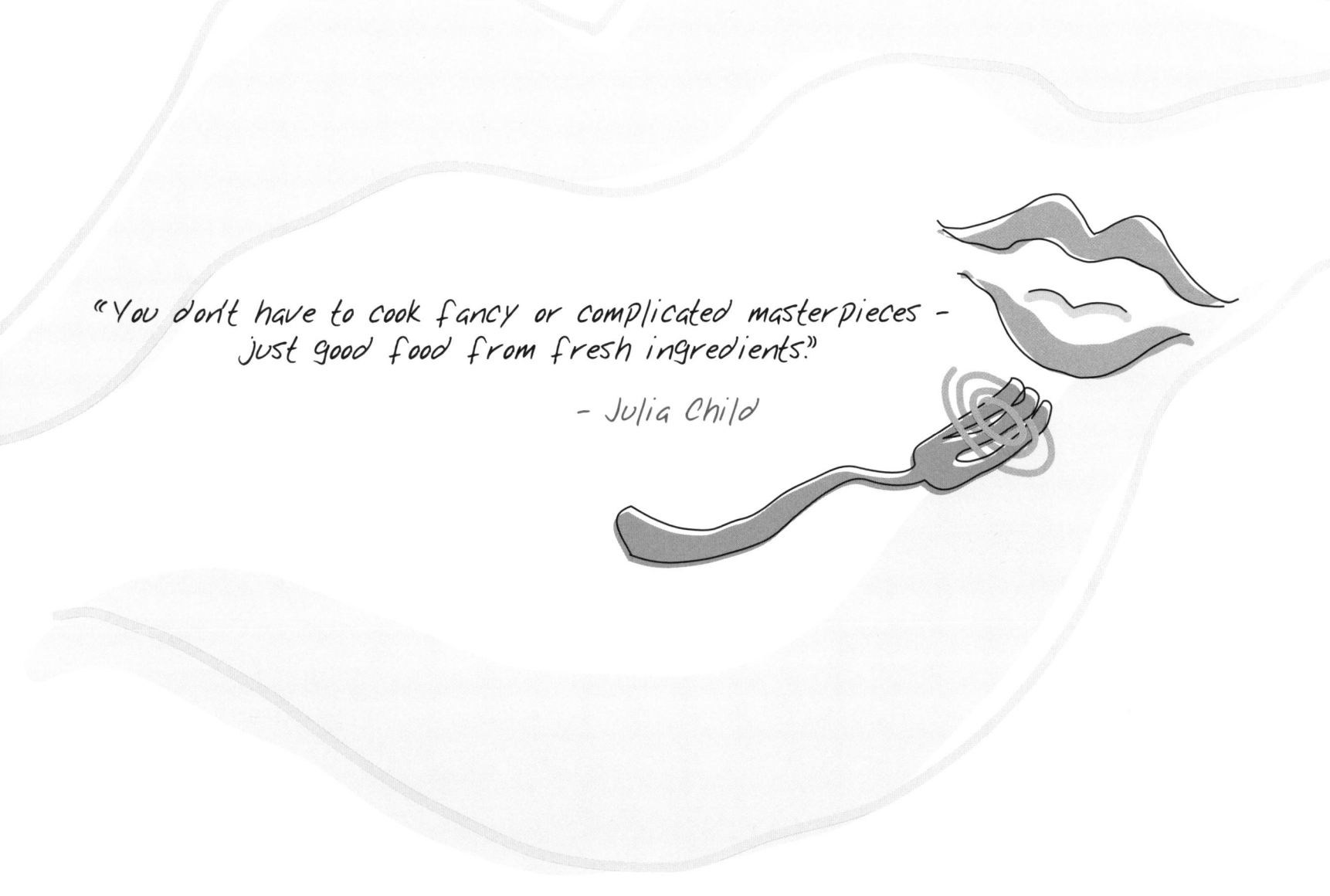

"You don't have to cook fancy or complicated masterpieces – just good food from fresh ingredients."

– Julia Child

PRODUCE	DAIRY	FROZEN	MISCELLANEOUS

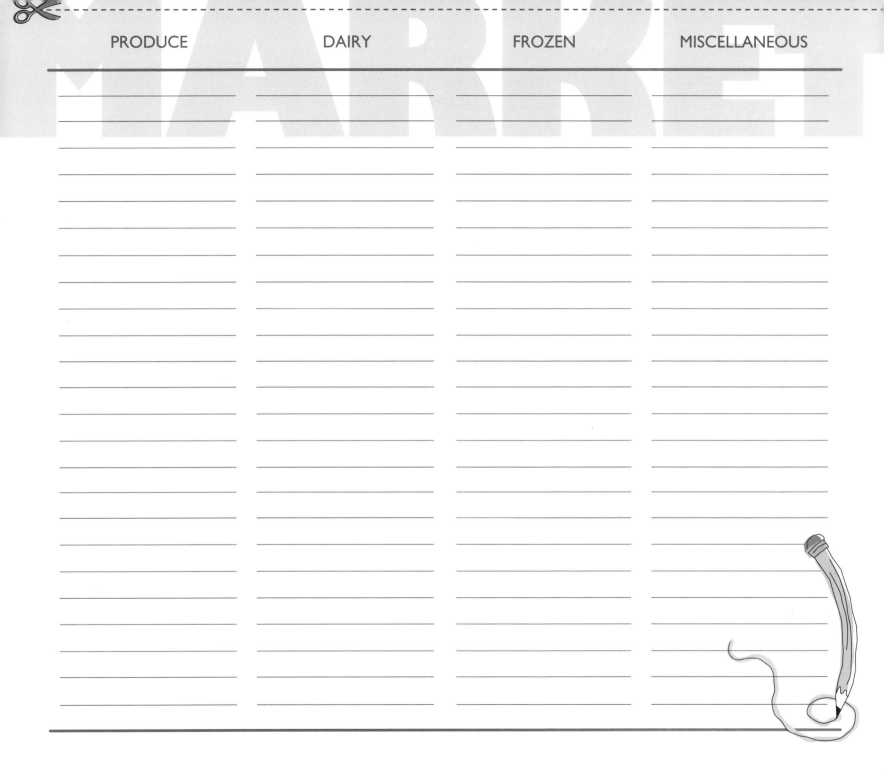

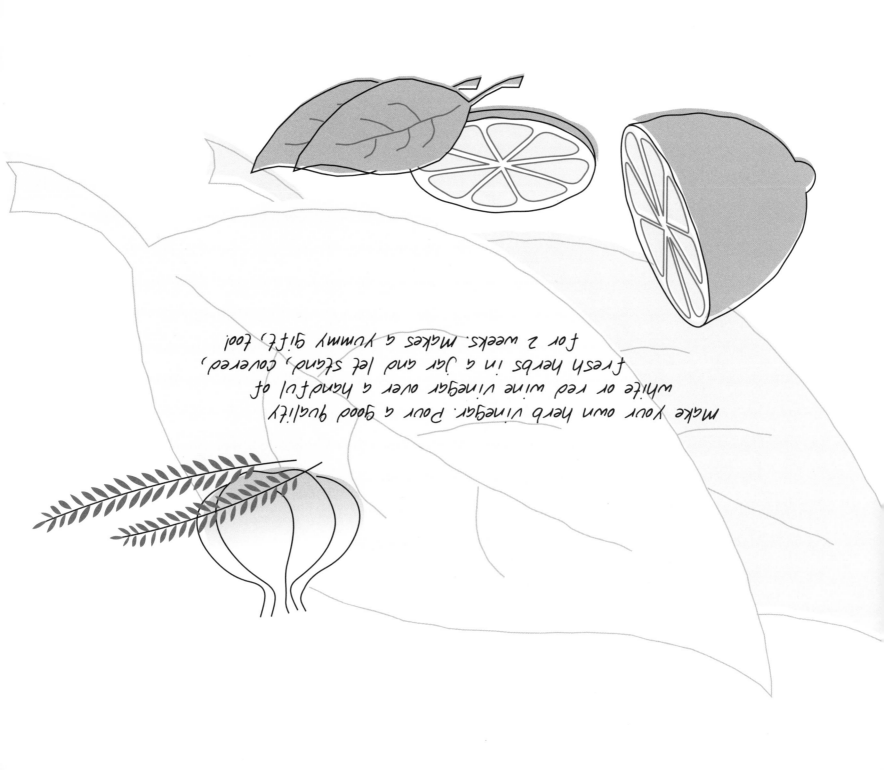

Make your own herb vinegar. Pour a good quality
white or red wine vinegar over a handful of
fresh herbs in a jar and let stand, covered,
for 2 weeks. Makes a yummy gift, too!

PRODUCE	DAIRY	FROZEN	MISCELLANEOUS

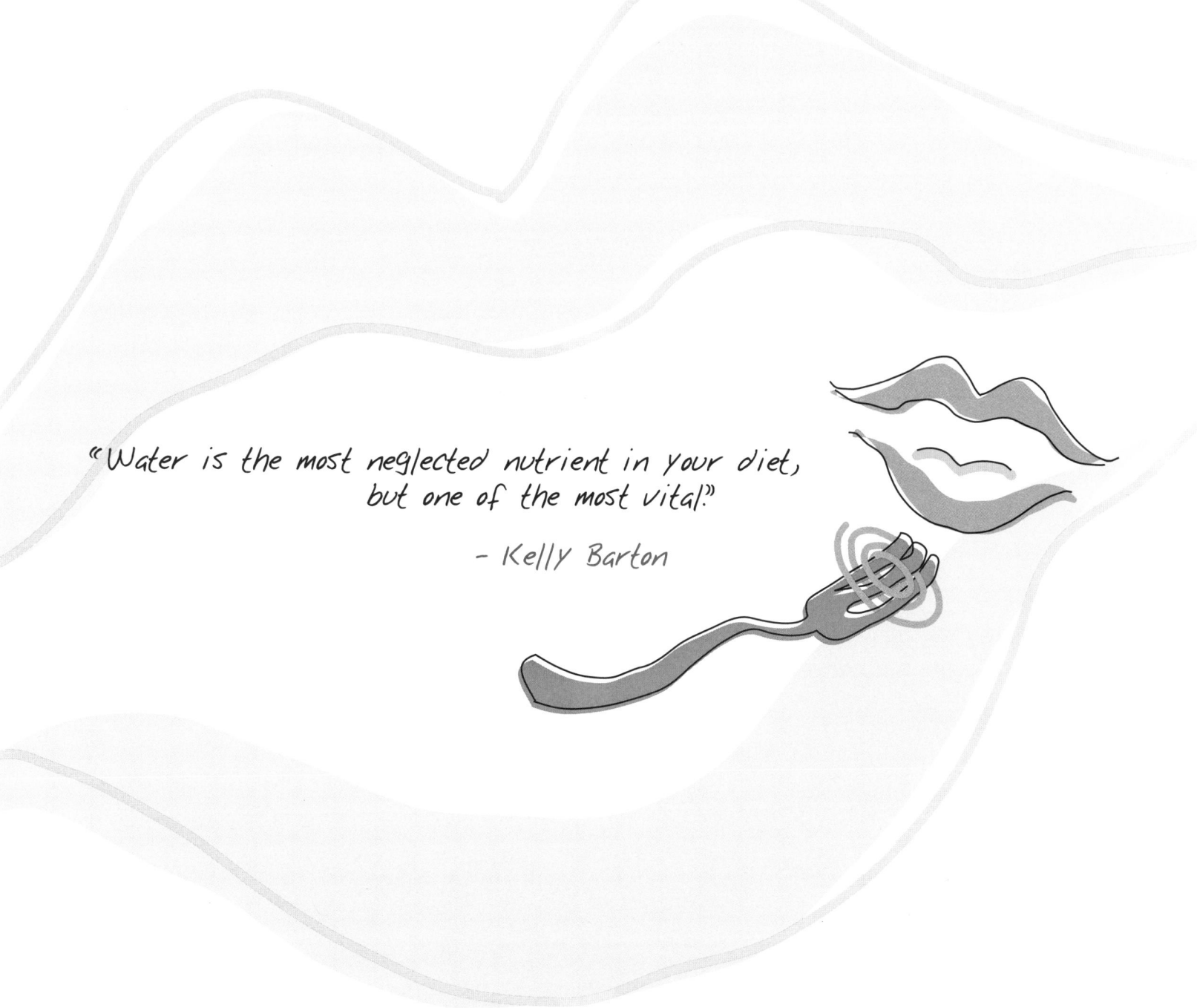

"Water is the most neglected nutrient in your diet,
but one of the most vital."

– Kelly Barton

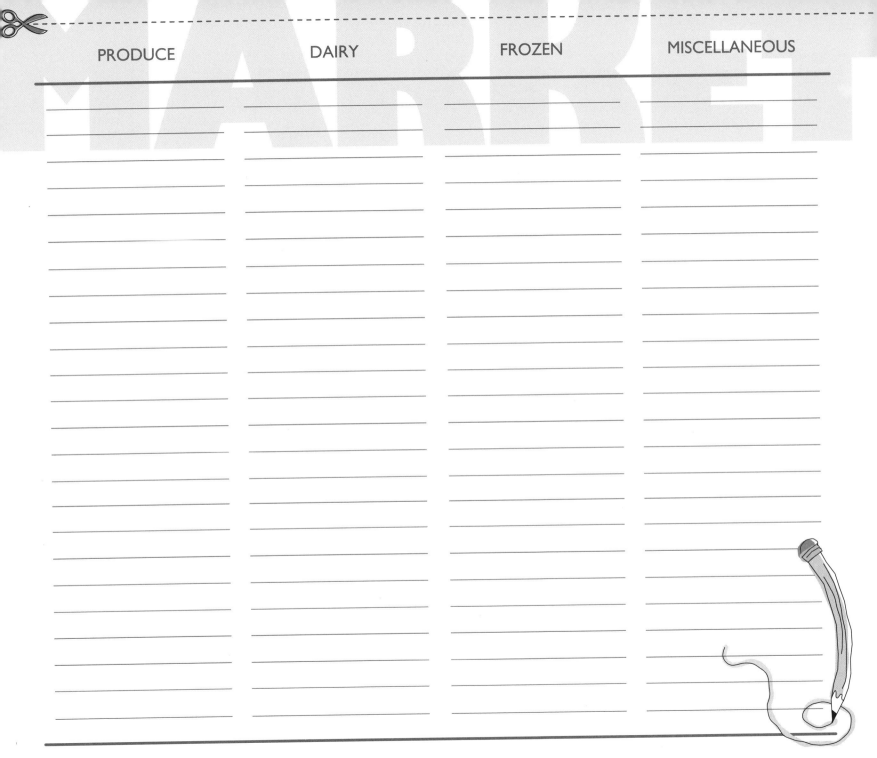

PRODUCE	DAIRY	FROZEN	MISCELLANEOUS

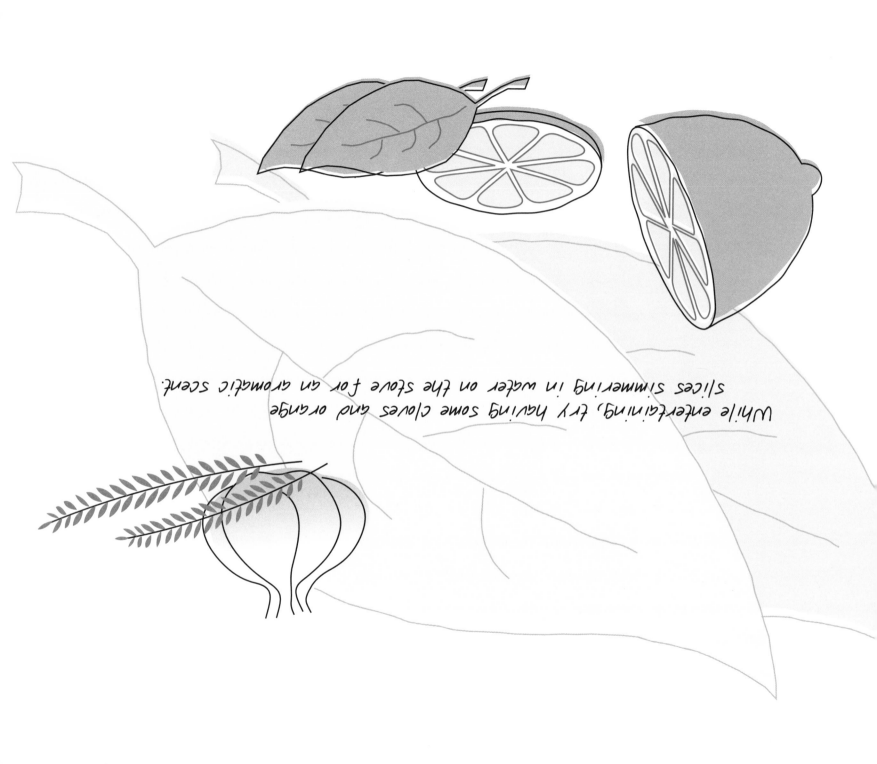

While entertaining, try having some cloves and orange slices simmering in water on the stove for an aromatic scent.

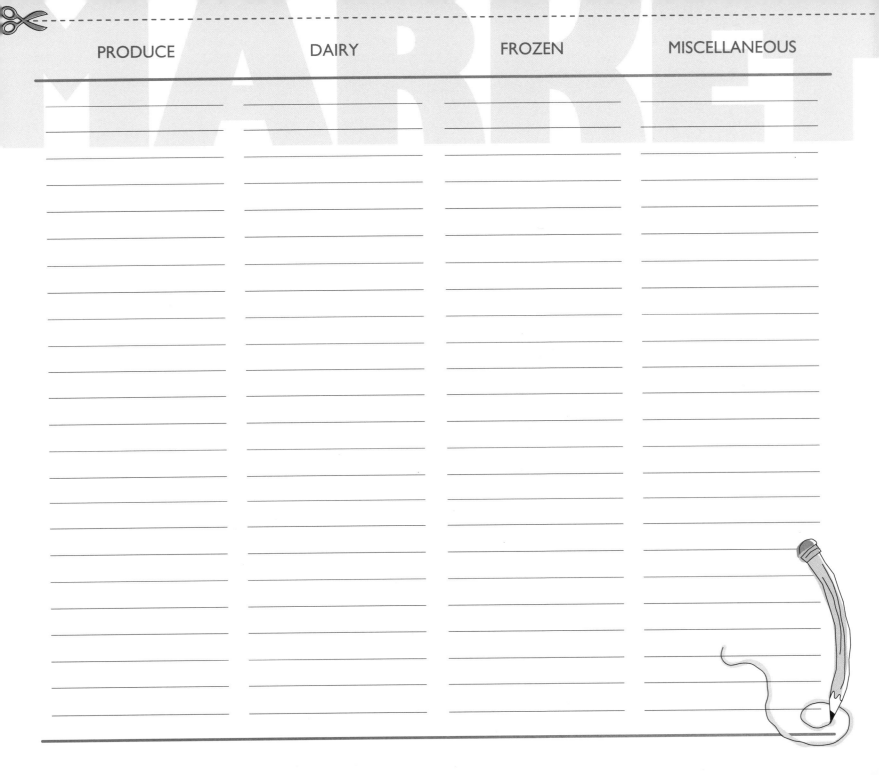

PRODUCE	DAIRY	FROZEN	MISCELLANEOUS

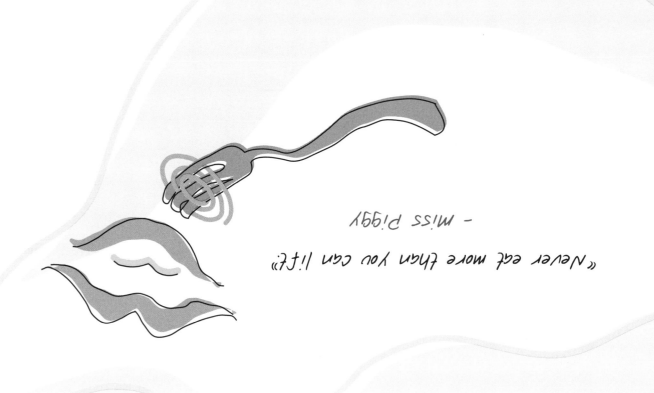

PRODUCE	DAIRY	FROZEN	MISCELLANEOUS

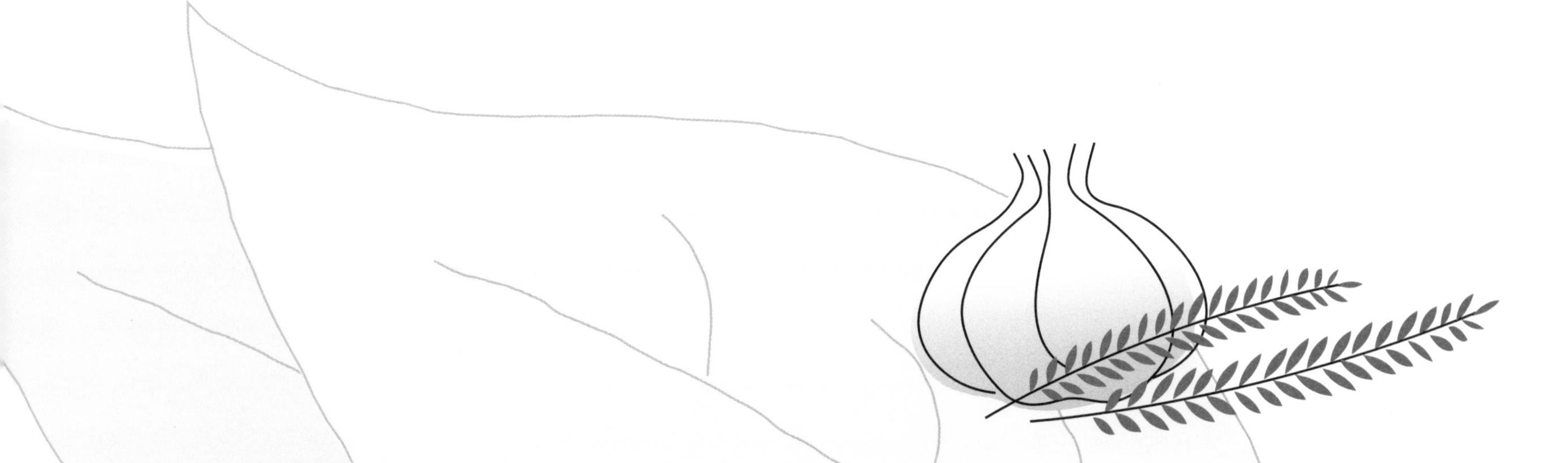

Dried herbs lose flavor rapidly when exposed to air, heat or light. Sniff jarred herbs occasionally. If there's no aroma, toss them. They won't do much for your recipe anyway.

PRODUCE	DAIRY	FROZEN	MISCELLANEOUS

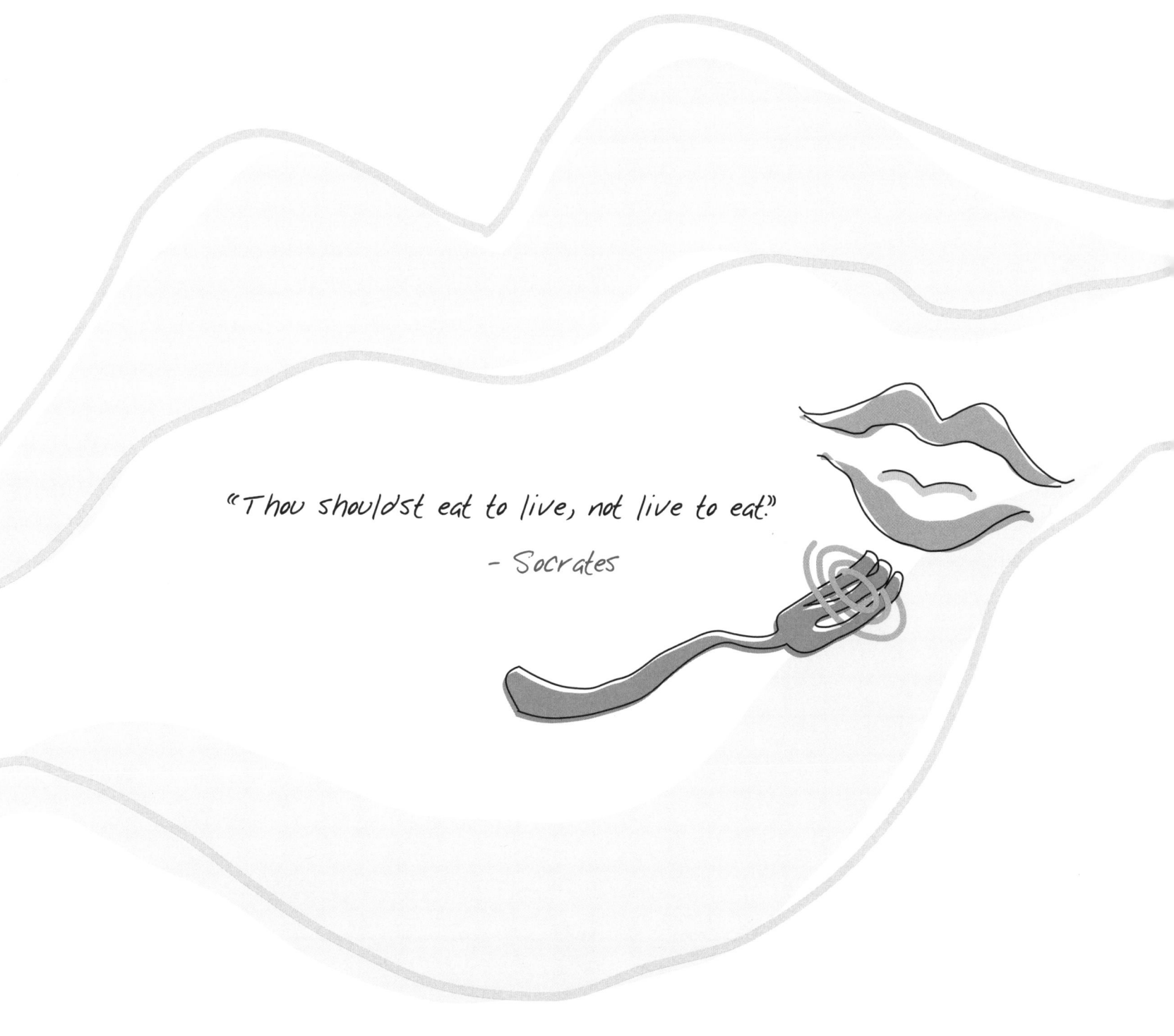

"Thou shouldst eat to live, not live to eat."

– Socrates

PRODUCE	DAIRY	FROZEN	MISCELLANEOUS

Adding a vanilla bean to your table sugar jar will
provide you with a delicious, aromatic treat for your
tea or coffee. Refill the jar with sugar as needed.

PRODUCE	DAIRY	FROZEN	MISCELLANEOUS

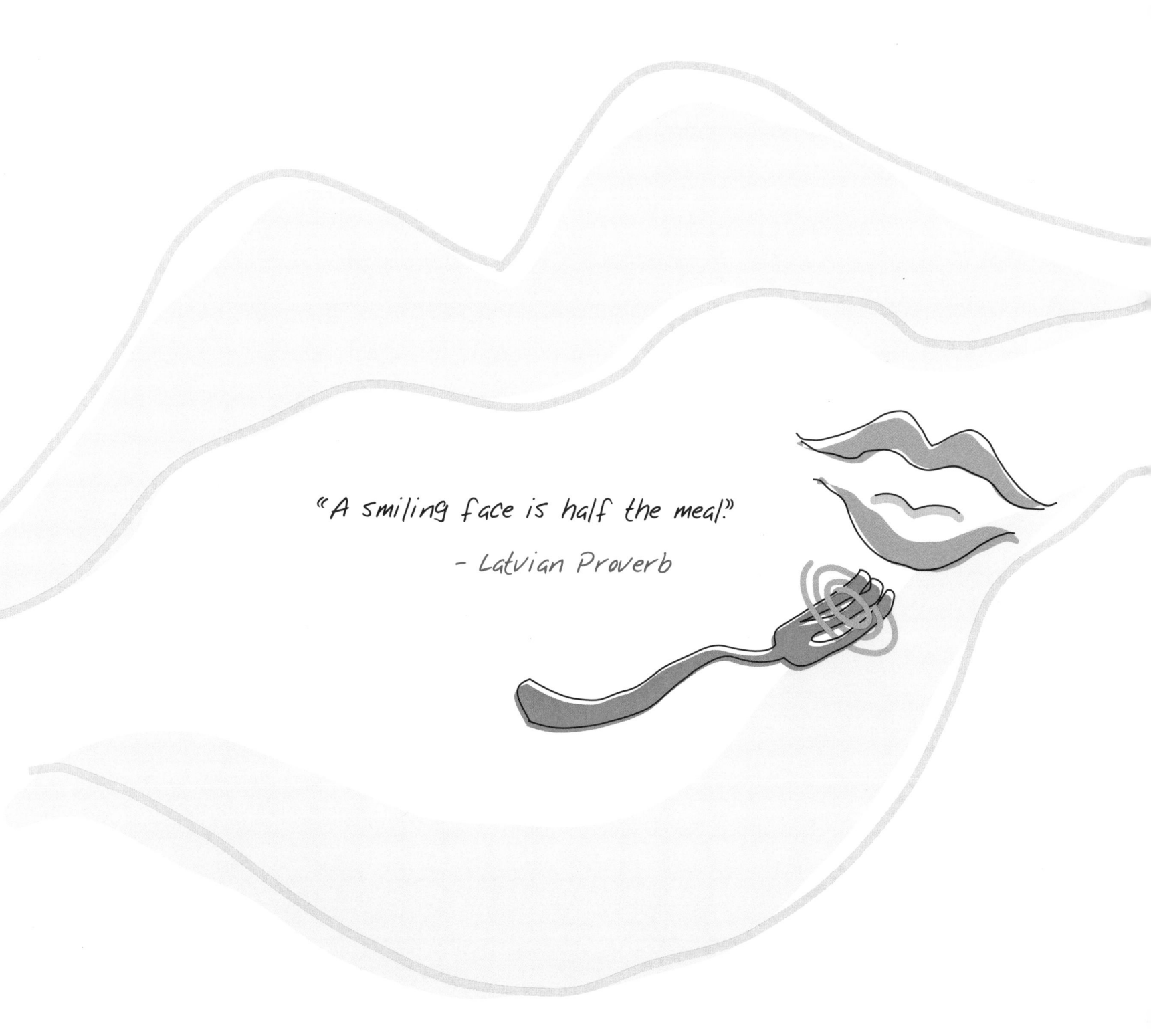

"A smiling face is half the meal."

- Latvian Proverb

PRODUCE	DAIRY	FROZEN	MISCELLANEOUS

Need a hostess gift? Fill a small mason jar with
bulk tea and tie a ribbon around the neck inexpensive,
as well as unique, practical and adorable!

PRODUCE	DAIRY	FROZEN	MISCELLANEOUS

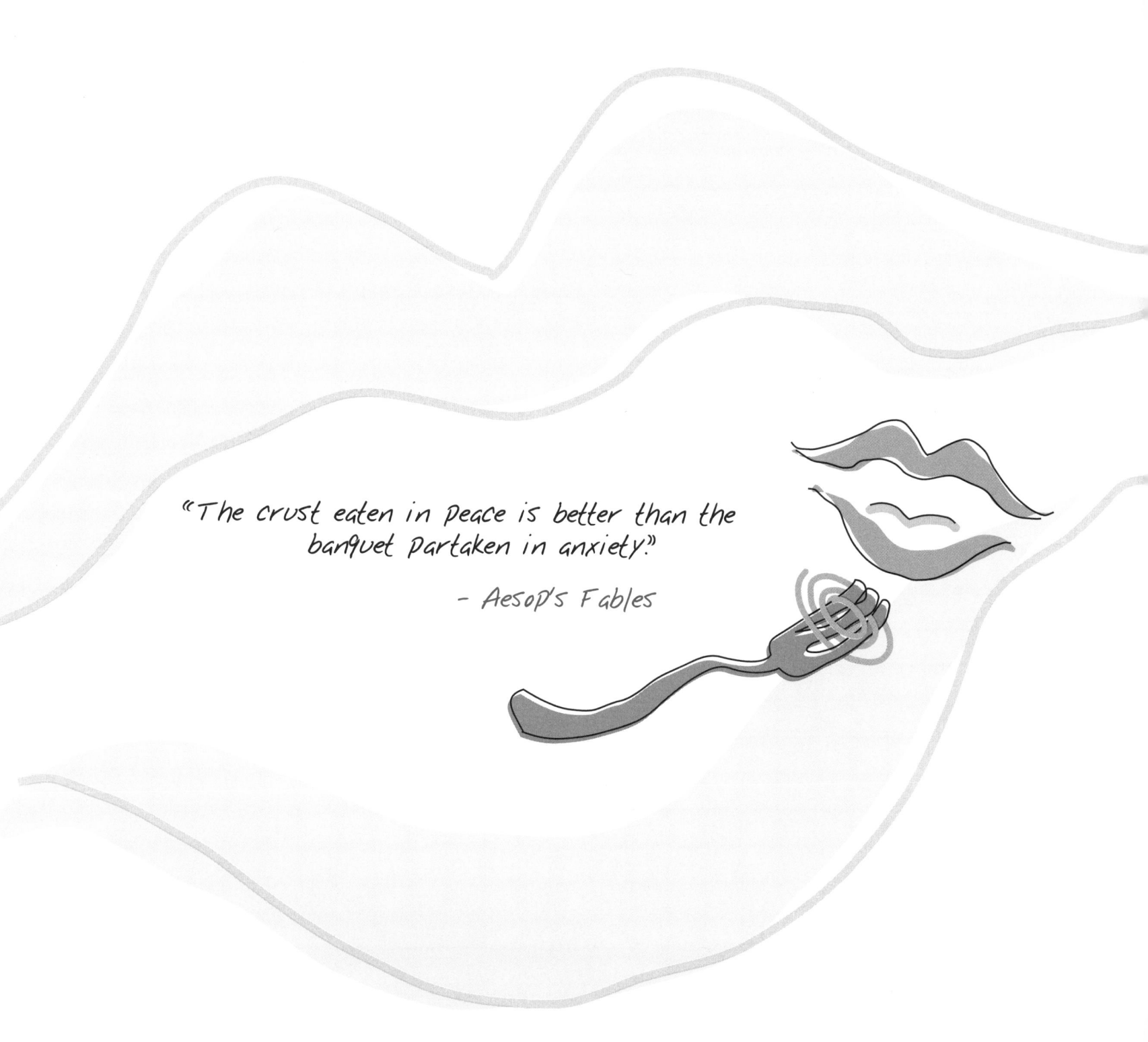

"The crust eaten in peace is better than the banquet partaken in anxiety."

– Aesop's Fables

PRODUCE	DAIRY	FROZEN	MISCELLANEOUS

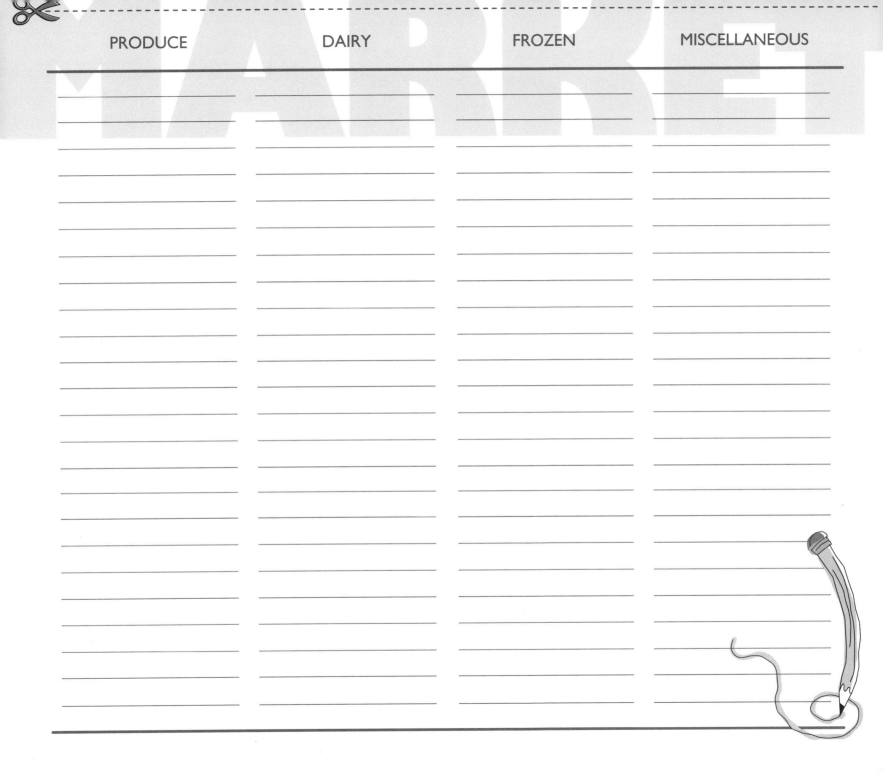

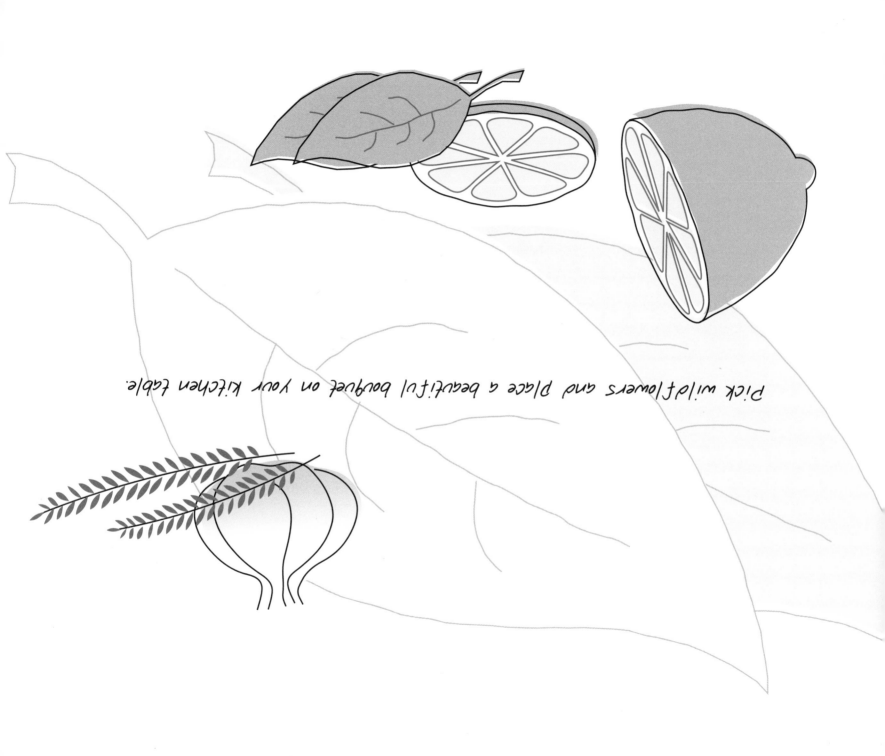

Pick wildflowers and place a beautiful bouquet on your kitchen table.

PRODUCE	DAIRY	FROZEN	MISCELLANEOUS

"One cannot think well, love well, sleep well,
if one has not dined well."

– Virginia Wolfe,
A Room of One's Own

PRODUCE	DAIRY	FROZEN	MISCELLANEOUS

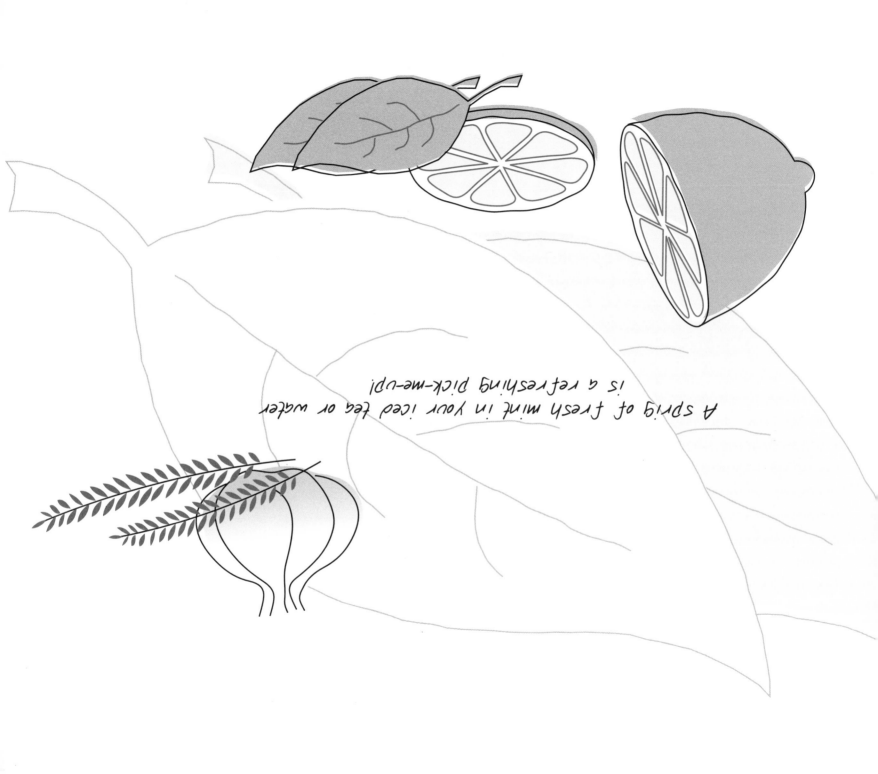

A sprig of fresh mint in your iced tea or water
is a refreshing pick-me-up!

PRODUCE	DAIRY	FROZEN	MISCELLANEOUS

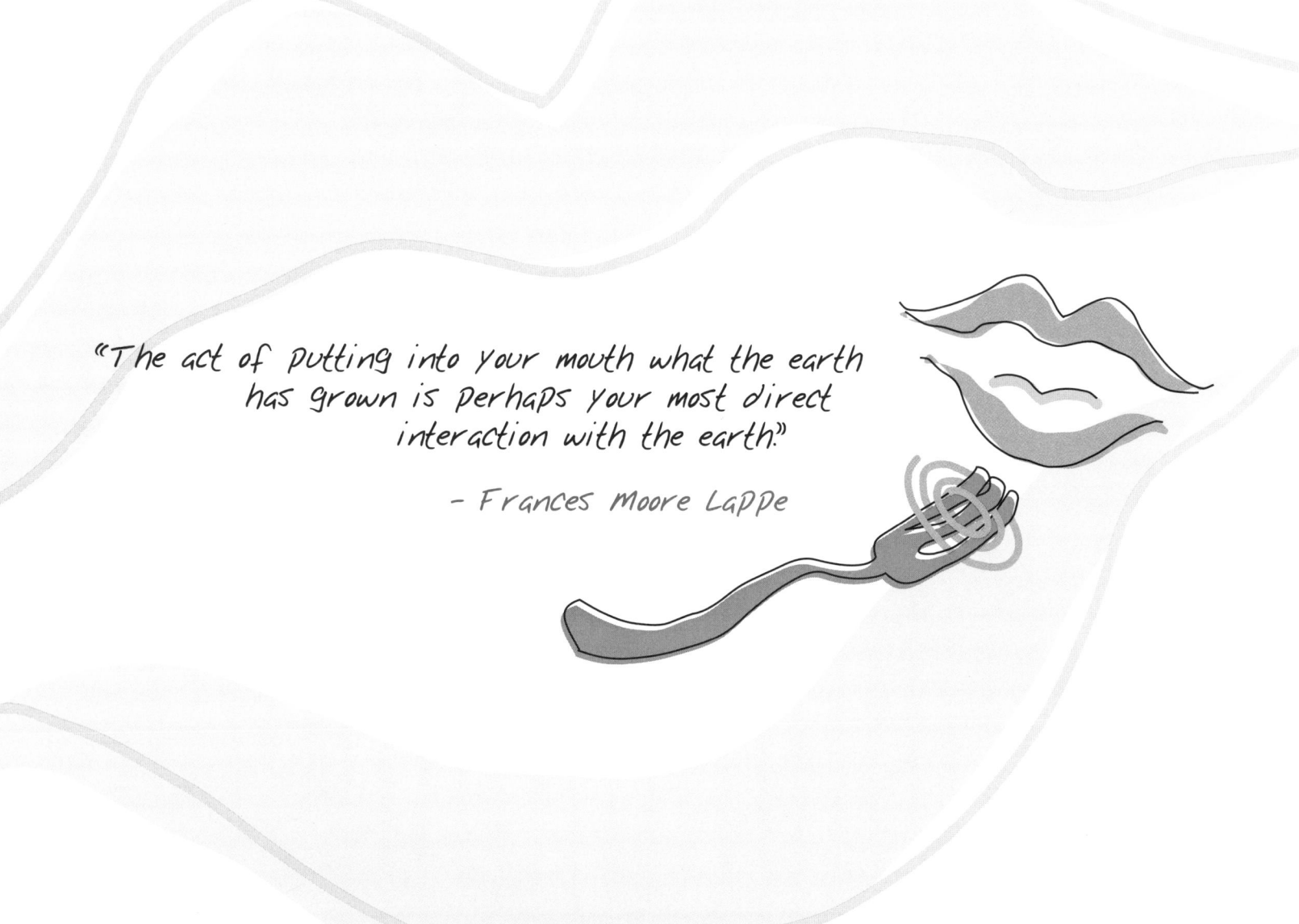

"The act of putting into your mouth what the earth has grown is perhaps your most direct interaction with the earth."

- Frances Moore Lappe

PRODUCE	DAIRY	FROZEN	MISCELLANEOUS

Instead of buying expensive fruit juice spritzers –
make your own! mix 1 part fruit juice with 3 parts
sparkling water in a glass over ice. voila! Healthy soda!

PRODUCE	DAIRY	FROZEN	MISCELLANEOUS

"Eating is not merely a material pleasure. Eating well gives a spectacular joy to life and contributes immensely to goodwill and happy companionship. It is of great importance to the morale."

– Elsa Schiaparelli

PRODUCE	DAIRY	FROZEN	MISCELLANEOUS

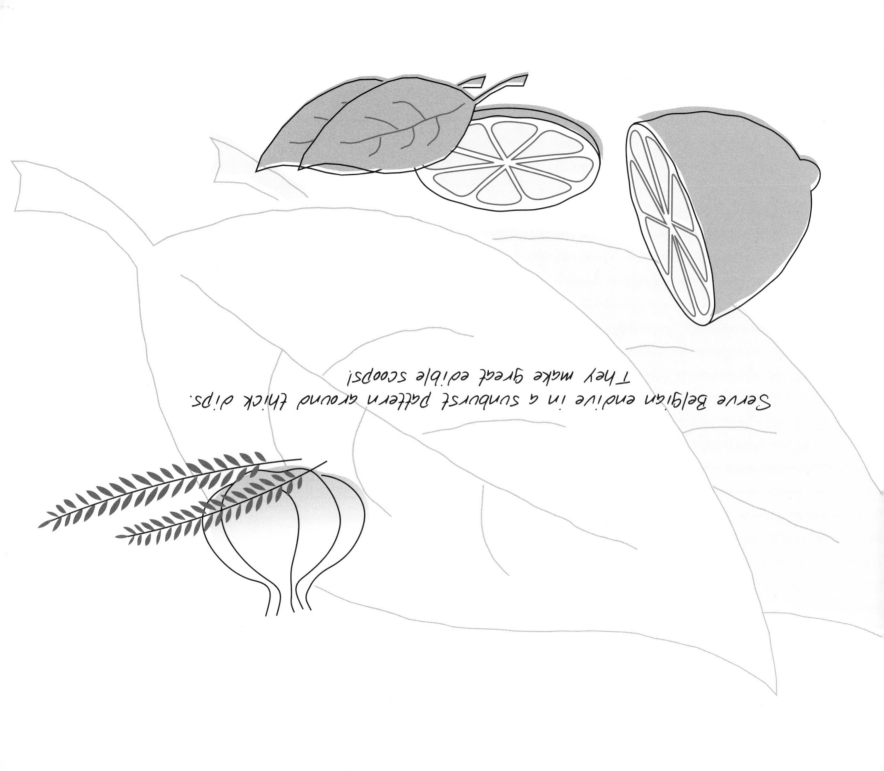

Serve Belgian endive in a sunburst pattern around thick dips. They make great edible scoops!

PRODUCE	DAIRY	FROZEN	MISCELLANEOUS

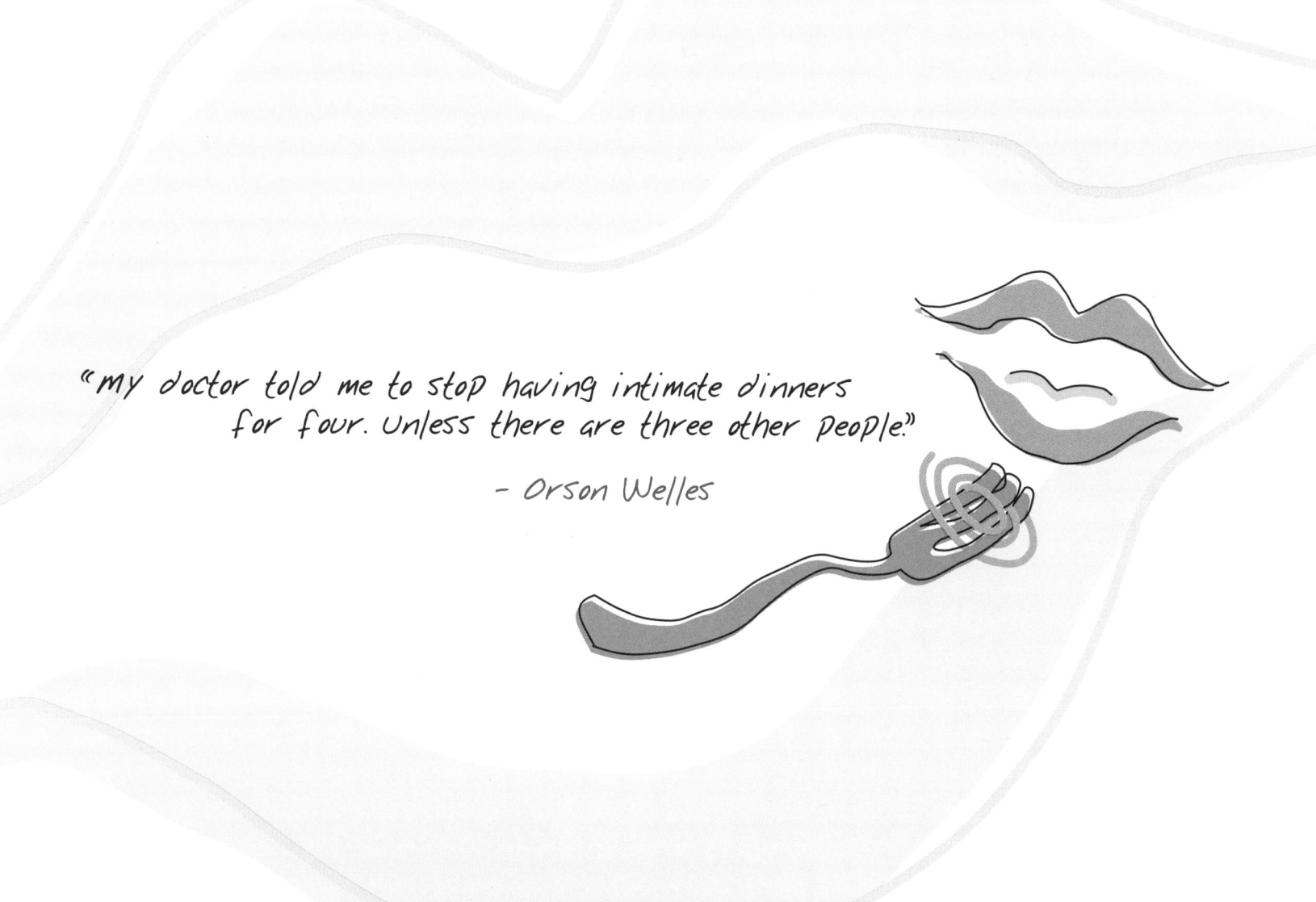

"my doctor told me to stop having intimate dinners
for four. Unless there are three other People."

– Orson Welles

PRODUCE   DAIRY   FROZEN   MISCELLANEOUS

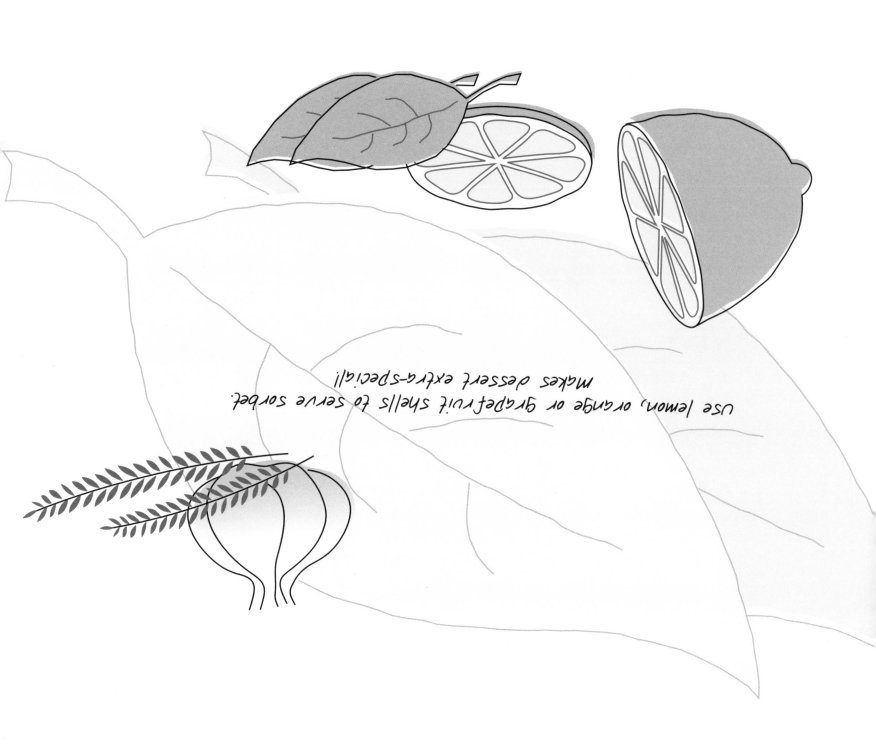

Use lemon, orange or grapefruit shells to serve sorbet. Makes dessert extra-special!

PRODUCE	DAIRY	FROZEN	MISCELLANEOUS

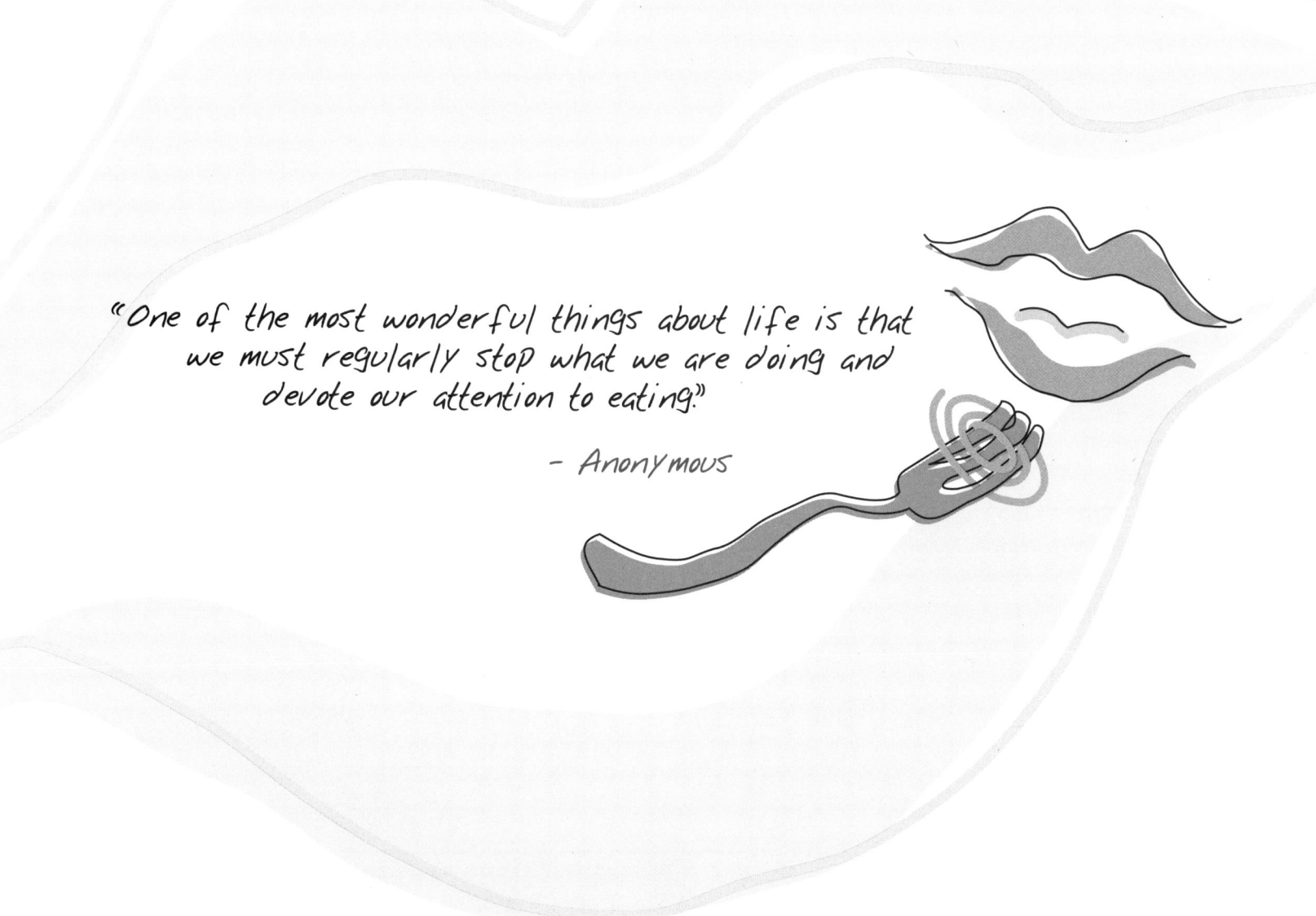

"One of the most wonderful things about life is that we must regularly stop what we are doing and devote our attention to eating."

– Anonymous

PRODUCE	DAIRY	FROZEN	MISCELLANEOUS

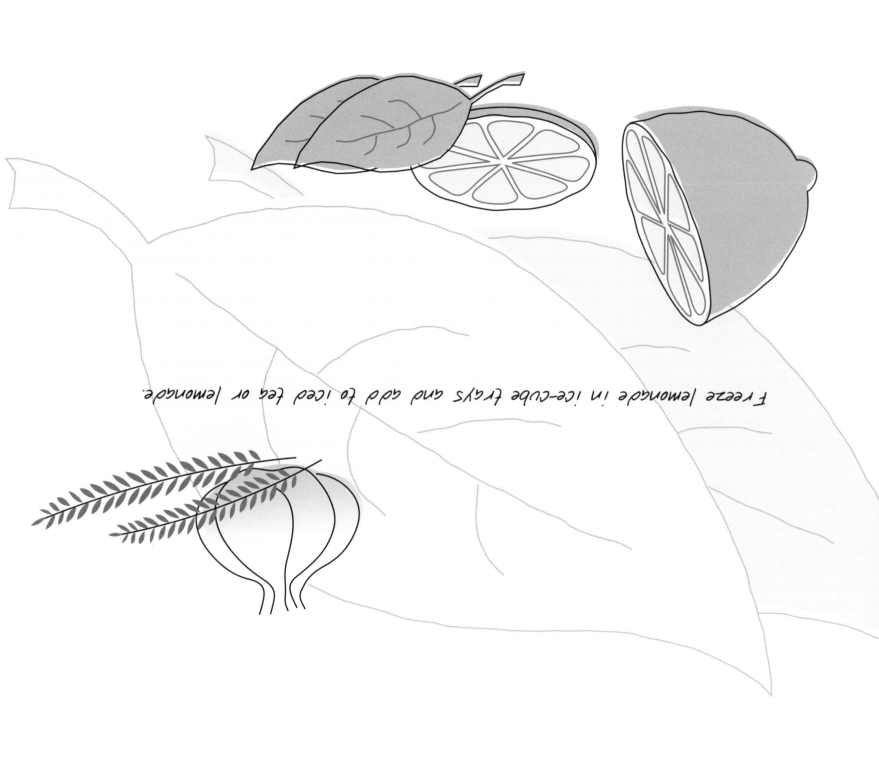

Freeze lemonade in ice-cube trays and add to iced tea or lemonade.

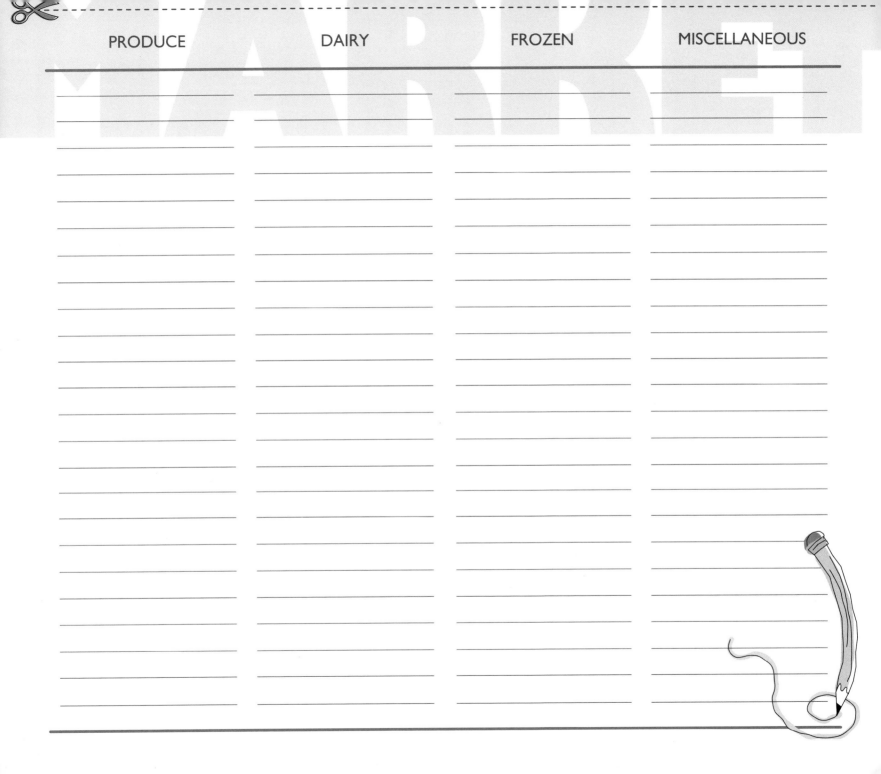

PRODUCE	DAIRY	FROZEN	MISCELLANEOUS

"No man is lonely while eating spaghetti – it requires too much attention."

– Christopher Morley

PRODUCE	DAIRY	FROZEN	MISCELLANEOUS

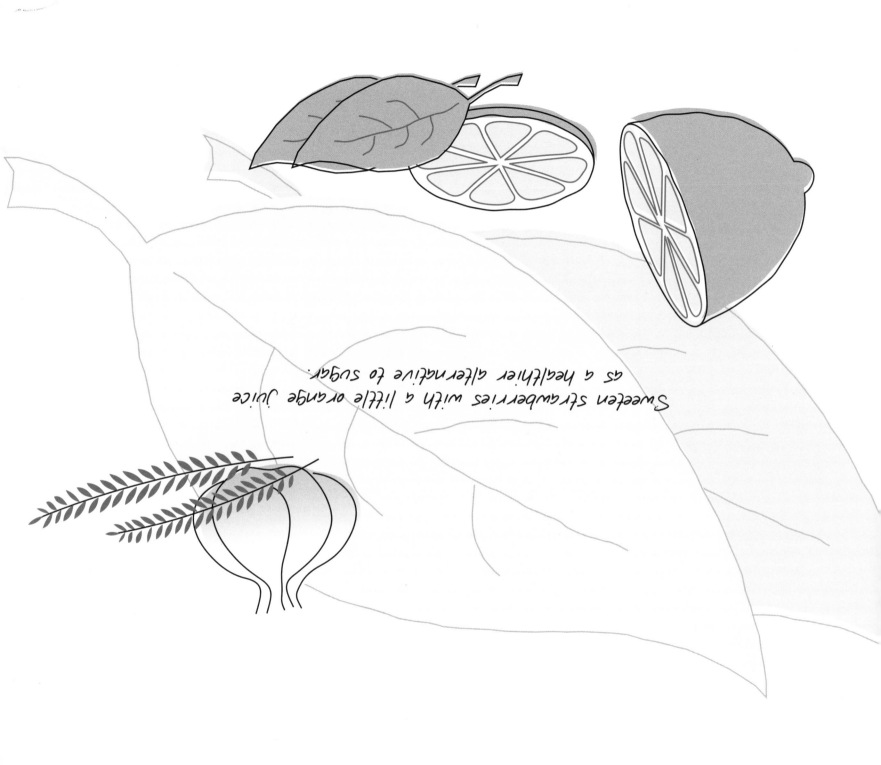

Sweeten strawberries with a little orange juice as a healthier alternative to sugar.

PRODUCE	DAIRY	FROZEN	MISCELLANEOUS

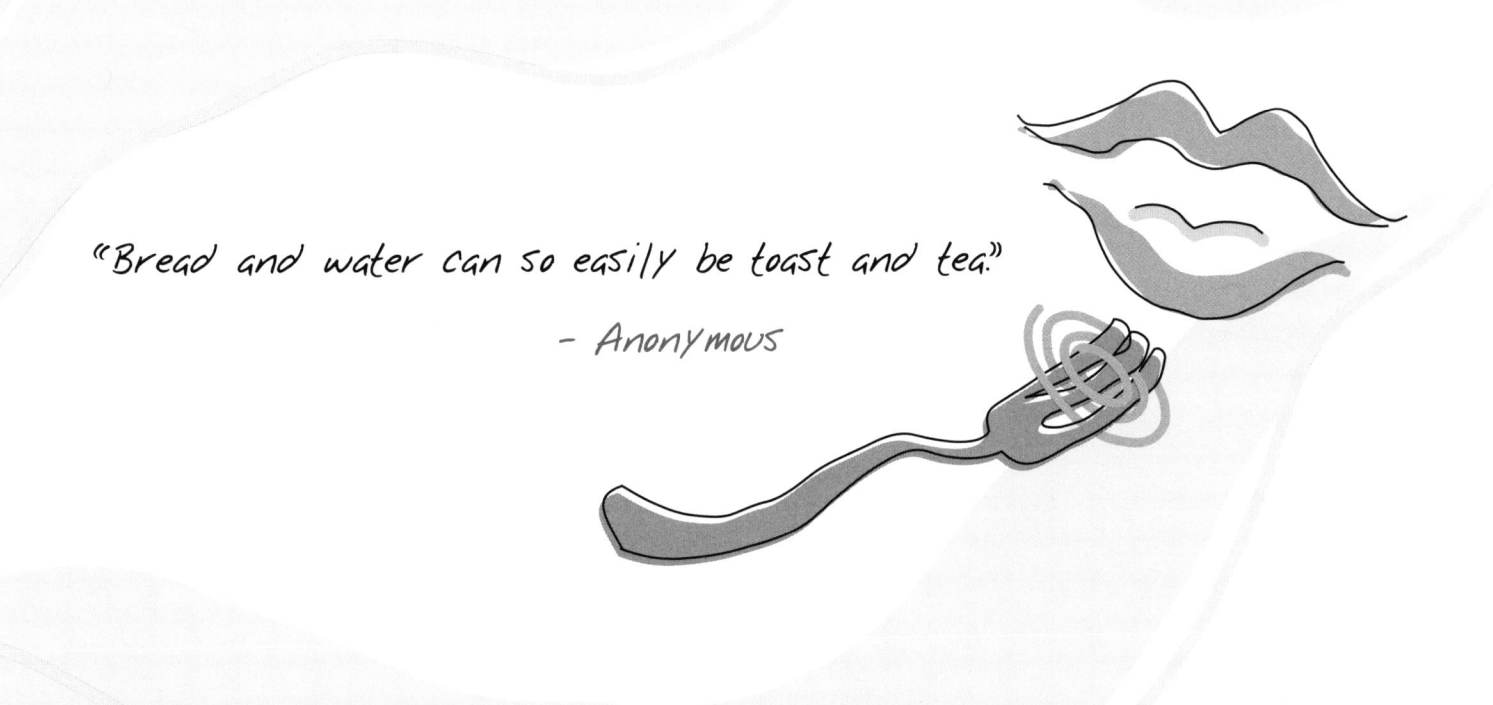

"Bread and water can so easily be toast and tea."

– Anonymous

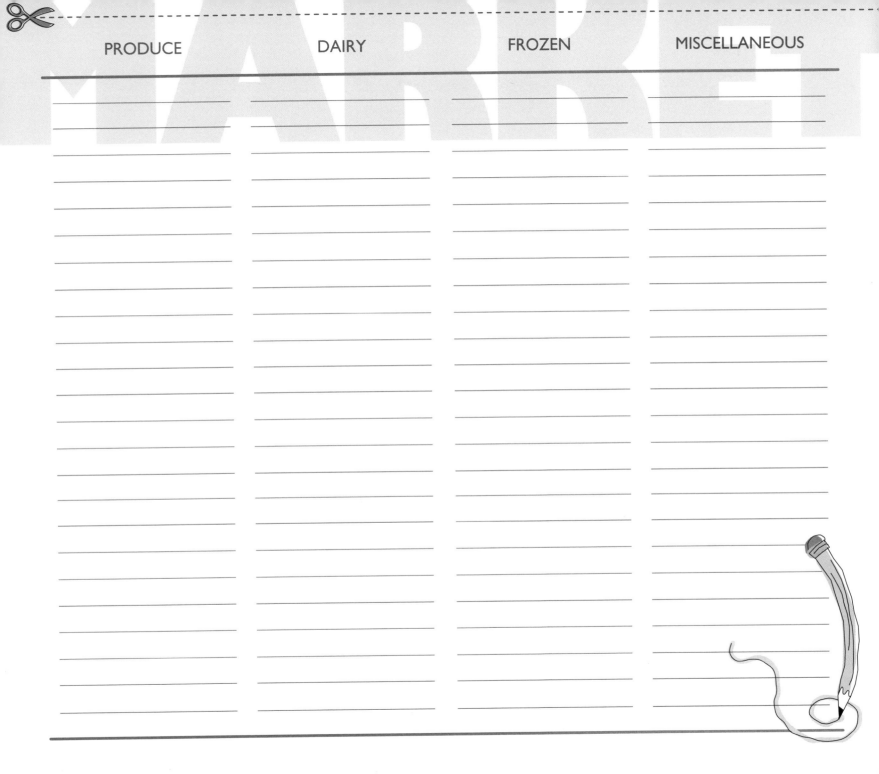

PRODUCE	DAIRY	FROZEN	MISCELLANEOUS

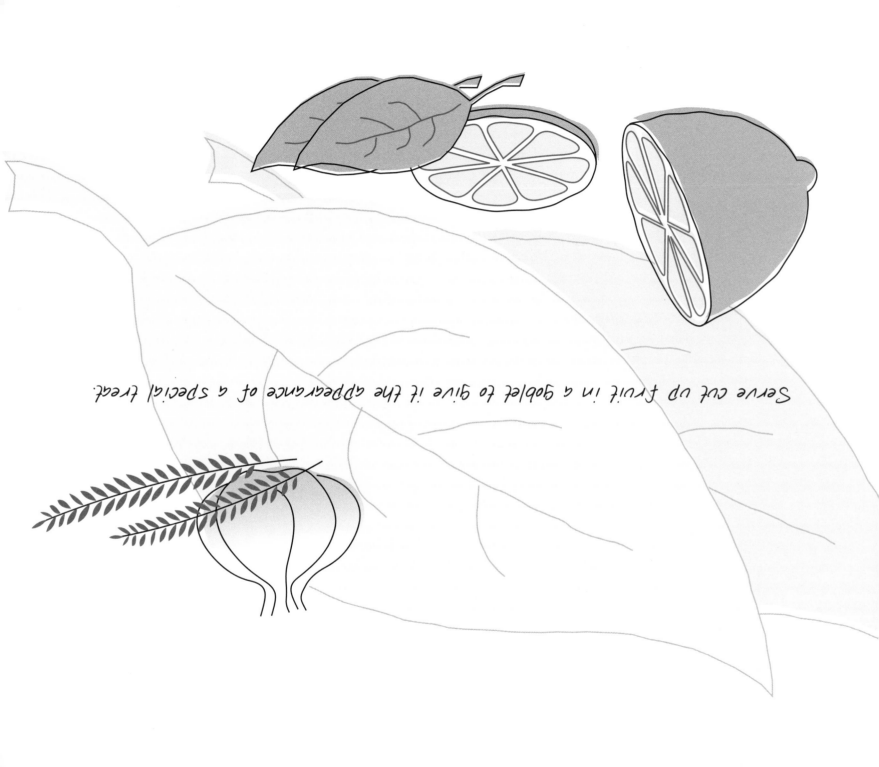

Serve cut up fruit in a goblet to give it the appearance of a special treat.

PRODUCE	DAIRY	FROZEN	MISCELLANEOUS

"Women are like tea bags. They don't know how strong they are until they get into hot water."

– Eleanor Roosevelt

PRODUCE	DAIRY	FROZEN	MISCELLANEOUS

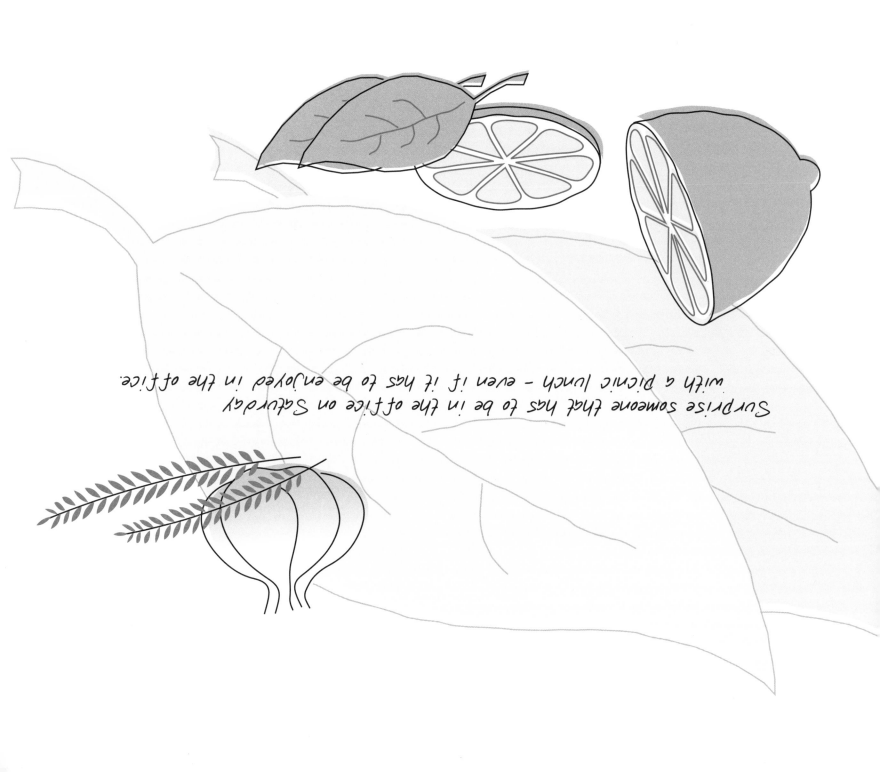

Surprise someone that has to be in the office on Saturday
with a picnic lunch - even if it has to be enjoyed in the office.

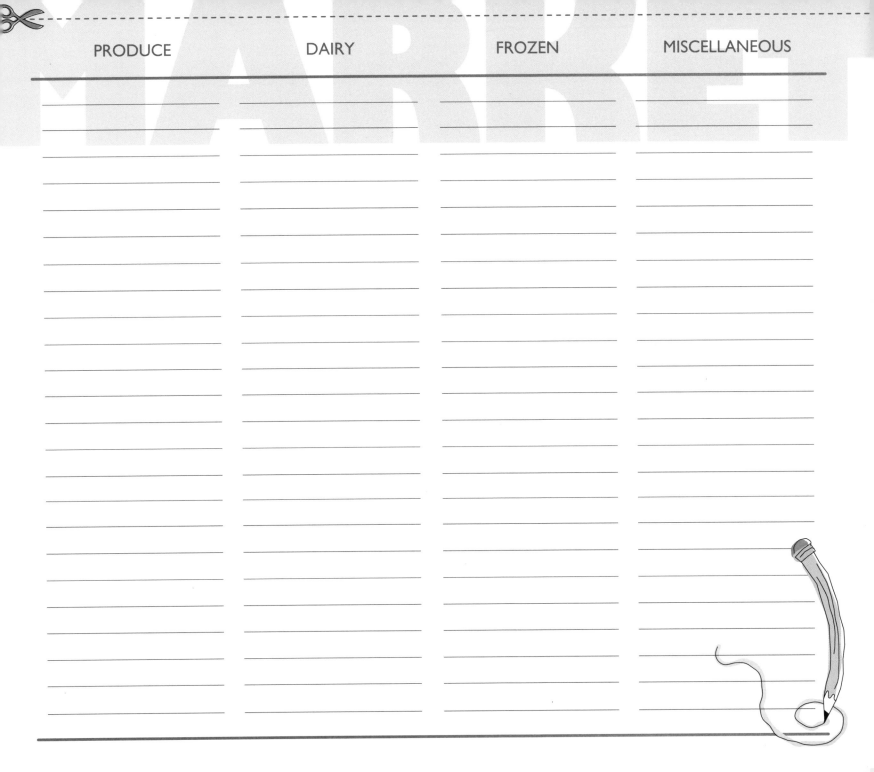

PRODUCE	DAIRY	FROZEN	MISCELLANEOUS

"Come let us have some tea and continue to talk about happy things."

— Chaim Potok, The Chosen

PRODUCE	DAIRY	FROZEN	MISCELLANEOUS